8/03

eddie campbell

After the snooter

eddie campbell books
2002

D1214927

AFTER THE SNOOTER

First printing June 2002
Published by Eddie Campbell Books
PO Box 230, Paddington QLD 4064, Australia.
Internet: http://www.eddiecampbellcomics.com
email: eddie@eddiecampbellcomics.com

After the snooter and all other material ™ and © Eddie Campbell 2002. All rights reserved. No portion
of this book may be reproduced by any means (excepting legitimate reasons of review) without express
permission from the copyright holders.

Book designed by Michael Evans.
PRINTED IN CANADA.
Available in the US from: Chris Staros,
Top Shelf Productions, PO Box 1282, Marietta GA 30061-1282.
Internet: http://www.topshelfcomix.com
ISBN 0 9577896 6 1

PUBLISHING HISTORY

The impetus for this book was provided by two unrelated commisssions in 1995 and 1996, one from
Dark Horse Presents for the special 100th issue which is now the opening chapter, the other from
Scottish newspaper **The Herald** for which I drew *The Forriners*. Each piece expressed a separate
theme which seemed unrelated but the two fused over the next few years in anecdotal discursions in
Bacchus Magazine until its demise in 2001. The work demanded a conclusion which appears for
the first time in this volume. In this book, I drop the pretence of being Alec MacGarry.

Other books by Eddie Campbell

Alec: The King Canute Crowd
Alec: How To Be An Artist
Alec: Three Piece Suit
From Hell *(with Alan Moore)*
The Birth Caul *(with Alan Moore)*
Snakes and Ladders *(with Alan Moore)*

St. Louis Community College
at Meramec
Library

A tale of horror
by
Eddie
Campbell
Feb 95

The Snooter buffered in on a humid night.

I was cleaning my empty bottle collection...

...like they were doing in the galley of the *Marie Celeste*

...on that dark and doleful day.

They too saw the sign.

I too failed to take heed...

...and felt only a sympathy for the creature.

The snooter had lodged himself down behind my archives.

I brought him to safety.

How did a thing so strange get to live to be so big...

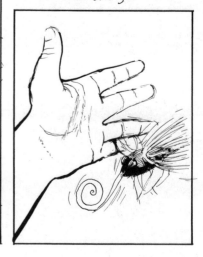

...in this, the age of the small poppy?

I watched the snooter depart, nevermore to see his nasal tendril...

...except for the next time, which was in Yocky's mouth.

The rash was not preceeded by any prediction...

"Leo: Mark time businesswise. Health average."

And it had this long tendril coming from its snout.

Are you sure you hadn't been drinking?

...or so wifey said. I don't follow the horoscopes.

My fingers look like porridge from days of auld lang syne.

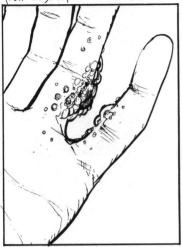

I have not been sleeping well for years.

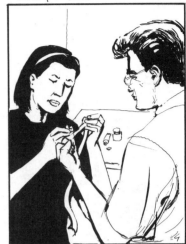

In the dark silence of night, all horrors are unwrapped.

Must warn the world.

Beware the Snooter

Eddie Campbell 10.00

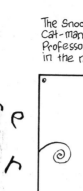

The Snooter next visited the Cat-man. He was a University Professor till one day he looked in the mirror and saw the Snooter.

He went down the road and set up house on a bench.

He licked himself while his family moved away and the house sat empty.

Months became years.

Once, the city council removed the bench, but there was a local murmur of complaint on the Cat-man's behalf.

The Cat-man got a new bench.

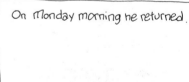

One Father's Day Sunday he was gone

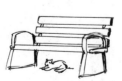

On Monday morning he returned.

Onward it flies, on its dark mission, the Snooter.

Many years ago, a couple wanted to go back to England but their kids didn't like the idea.

They'd already sold up the house and were in a hotel *en route* to flying out when they changed their minds and decided to stay.

They returned to their country town and rented a house on the street where they had lived.

Eventually their old house came up for sale and they bought it again.

The daughter's course through life was not marred by any untoward event; worked as a secretary for a local small business for twenty five years after leaving school, married for twenty years, chose to have no children.

One Tuesday evening while driving to visit her parents at 6.30. as she had done every Tuesday evening, she saw a strange shadow in a dark side street.

She went home and hung herself in the bathroom.

After the Snooter...

11/9/99

Eddie Campbell

...everything is different. Not necessarily chronologically, like "before and after" pictures of cellulite, but I look back and realize that somewhere around that time, before or after, I became another person.

It's one of Ms. Sheehy's life-"passages" I suspect. Everyone starts glancing sideways to see if one's fellows are alongside, or ahead, or behind.

> Richard said he met a man yesterday of his own age, who has three real estate investment properties and it made him assess what he's achieved with his life so far.

The information comes to me like that, indirectly. Nobody will tell me straight, either because they don't talk straight at all or because they think I'm a piss-taker and I'll put it in a comic and laugh at it.

> Ha Ha ha! and that's his idea of what's important.?

I notice that suddenly I'm open to suggestions

> I wake up in the awful dark with the terrors of the infinite upon me.

> Have you thought of giving up the drink?

And sensitive to comments

> Dad. Milhouss hair's going grey just like yours, starting at the back

> MILLY MOOMOO

I find myself, unusually, looking back down the road all the way to school. The new music teacher favoured me for some reason. I was not great at music, or any other subject, except for art of course.

I played the violin. Never with enthusiasm. And was uncomfortable about the un-coolness of it. Of course nobody ever said 'cool' except Ice Cool on West Side Story.

> Go Cooly coo boy

There were outings to the opera. I had nothing in common with the other guys here. But then, I didn't have much in common with anyone.

My anti-social adolescence manifests itself in the solitariness of artistic pursuit.

Anthony, you're up here on your own too much. Why don't you come and watch TV with us?

Later, mum.

It's difficult to be objective, of course, but in memory's mirror I see a good-looking kid, painfully shy, but with a surprising certainty about his destination in life. Needs to wash more often.

One evening I turn up for one of those operatic outings to find I'm the only boy there. The school music teacher's taking me to the opera.

It happened more than once.

Thanx

I sympathised with his anguish as the jackals of 4B(2) routinely tore pieces off him and he didn't appear to have any kind of survival instinct.

Yes, well sometimes. Popular music can be good. The crooners for instance...

Fuckin crooners ha ha!

He took his frustration out on me once and I could see his immediate and painful regret.

Oh ED-WARD YOO-HOO

Edward

I presume the pack explained away to themselves his slip of familiarity as resulting from being a family friend or something like that, otherwise they'd have been shredding me up too.

For a bookworm I seem to have garnered an odd amount of jackal-respect, without ever being mentally present enough to care about seeking jackal-favour.

Let me nick it for ya

I think you would too

I just bought myself a violin.

What? We've been together fifteen years and I didn't even know you could read music.

First there was the Snooter and then there was Sim. The Silver Surfer and Galactus. The Canadian's in this part of the world for a show in Sydney and comes up for a big hello.

You're planting your seeds all over the place like Little Johnny Appleseed. It would be okay if somebody was watering them.

No. He's been sent here. The show is irrelevant. The agent sent from the other side usually knows what his business is. He's delivering a package of information.

You've just got to rechannel all your energy and I'll tell you how.

To repeat the information here of course would be foolish. It comes encrypted in language so simple that I spend five days laughing.

We're in a hotel suite for that time ostensibly doing a little throwaway collaboration.

The Fire hose reel!

FIRE HOSE REEL

He ends on an odd note:

And one last thing, Johnny Appleseed... Never bore your god.

Later he gets religion. I don't know who delivers his package.

I leave him to recuperate and catch his plane out. Back home my confidence dissipates with Sim's smoke after I open my bag.

I run it past my father when I'm in England.

I'm thinking of becoming my own publisher.

Isn't that a bit risky, son?

Well, how am I making my living now? I say. I make up stories then get on the phone and try to sell them. I mention my plan to one of my American editors.

I'm thinking of becoming my own publisher.

Surely this is a bad time, the way the market's going.

A couple of months later, a brain tumor is diagnosed and within the year the poor guy's dead. What is risk? By that time I'm already my own publisher. I should have done it ten years ago.

New Year's Eve I'm sitting on the veranda with Annie and a bottle of Champagne. The kids're asleep.

We call Little old Nell over to have a glass with us. But after ten minutes she spies a more interesting proposition up the road. Even little old ladies have got better places to be. I'm crestfallen

what I need is a new gang.

So I dig out the mail I've been getting for my magazine, the local ones.

There's this guy who gift-wrapped a bottle of speckled Hen and left it for me at the comic shop.

Then there's this guy... 'Campbell! You're a fuckin' amateur... give me a call or...'

I arrange to meet them all at a pub at the same time. It goes off without a hitch. I introduce everybody to everybody else. Instant gang.

A crowd for Saturday afternoon beers, New Year's Eve singalongs, 'dambusters' (a game in which you clench coins in your buttocks)

Dress balls with Pride of Erin and all that.

My 40th Birthday party.

And I still wake in the dark night with the Snooter staring down at me. I stare right back at the bastard.

Now, what else needs changing?

T.he FOrriners

Eddie Campbell 11-97

"YOU WEANS GET OFF THE MONUMENT! WHAT WID YER GRANDFEATHER THINK O' IT?"

Brisbane, Australia.
A notion plants itself in my noggin.

Annie, I fancy taking a peek at the old school when we're back in Glasgow next week.

What's brought this on? You've always called it the 'Crypt of Terror'.

School. The régime instilled such a dread of the adult world being as miserable as the school one; that it was a relief to get a job in a factory where I was at least at liberty to daydream.

Ah, "we've all passed a lot of water since then".

It's just that I came across a picture of the building in this Architectural book: Glasgow: A Victorian City.

"An unusual building, this school catches the eye in a dismal stretch of Duke Street. The frontage is impressive... Six medallions with carved heads above the arches of the collonnade. They include Homer, Shakespeare, Milton".

And you never noticed before?

Guess I never looked up much. Hey! You lot put some clothes on, we're going out in a minute!

Comes the day. As always I work as I go, writing on the backs of envelopes and other scraps for Annie to type later.

Daddy, I don't want to stay in this house any more

Well we can't leave it for a while yet.

Manchester. The hired car is waiting. Annie's driving it. There's another thing I never got around to learning I was always the monomaniac: Fiercely focused on the one thing to the exclusion of all else.

Like those good dependable qualifications "to fall back on" I could never see any benefit in planning to fall over. They'll talk you out of being an artist, whatever it takes.

This is the first time the kids have come along on a trip. It's a chance for them to meet the grandparents as well as getting a few morsels of education themselves.

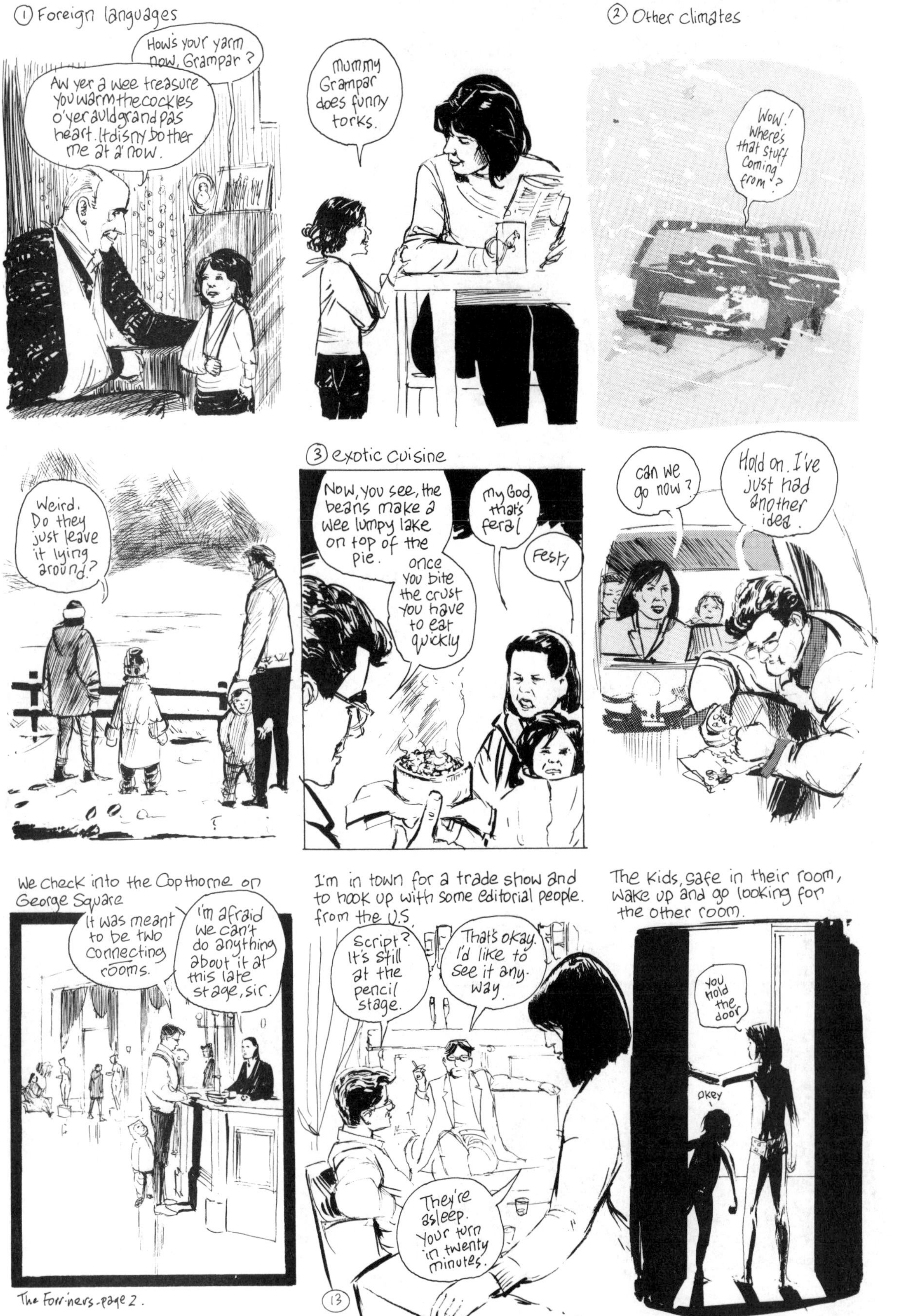

1 Foreign languages
How's your yarm now, Grampar?
Aw yer a wee treasure you warm the cockles o'yer auld grandpas heart. It disny bother me at a' now.
Mummy Grampar does funny torks.
2 Other climates
Wow! Where's that stuff coming from?
Weird. Do they just leave it lying around?
3 exotic cuisine
Now, you see, the beans make a wee lumpy lake on top of the pie.
once you bite the crust you have to eat quickly
my God, that's feral
Festy
can we go now?
Hold on. I've just had another idea.
We check into the Copthorne on George Square
It was meant to be two connecting rooms.
I'm afraid we can't do anything about it at this late stage, sir.
I'm in town for a trade show and to hook up with some editorial people from the U.S.
Script? It's still at the pencil stage.
That's okay. I'd like to see it anyway.
They're asleep. Your turn in twenty minutes.
The kids, safe in their room, wake up and go looking for the other room.
You hold the door
Okey
The Forriners-page 2.

Dear Grammar
Old men yell at us ol the time in Glasger

There it is. See what you think and I'll get it back tomorrow.

It's a few days before I remember to see the old *Alma Mater.*

A feeling of unease grips me as we cross High Street into Duke, just as it always did long ago

Twenty five years have not softened the severity of those chiselled features under judgemental white wigs. I hear their voices; Homer, Aristotle, Michelangelo and the rest.

The Forriners - page 3.

(14)

On the Street Where I lived

Wee Eddie Campbell
6/99.

There was a big woods behind the houses. Well, it seemed big to him when he lived there.

He had a recurring heroic half-dream where he was in a flat box go-cart, a wheeled wardrobe, I suppose, with mounted guns, hurtling down the slope, taking out the jerries, or teddy boys, or proddies...

BUDDA BUDDA

...whoever they were. Something to do with Rangers versus Celtic, he guessed, but it bewildered him later that nobody knew what he was talking about and neither did he.

Proddy dogs

FENIANS!

He became more introverted as he proceeded, watching the world go by from the dormer window of another house in another street.

dreaming of glugging wine in the Café Guerbois with the Impressionists.

making oil painting after oil painting, hundreds of them. He's scumbling down Cadmium street, brushing up against his heroes, greeting them with impasto.

Bong Zhoor Msieu Campbell

The paintings pile up. He's cataloguing them in the certainty that a historian will be travelling back this way.

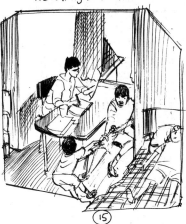

Then he throws them all in the bin one day when the bubble bursts.

Aw, no... and those ones of Grandma too?

So many young hopefuls lose that notion in the face of overwhelming odds. Who will ever count them?

"But what's the point of going to the academy to do Art? You can do that in your spare time."

The daydreaming student does not know how he got to start on the top level: class 1A(1). That means 1A in League Division One.

"CAMPBELL! WHY TWO TABLETS OF STONE?"

"eh? uh..nmm..Because there wasn't any paper back then?"

HA HA HI HI.

League Division Two's in another building several streets away. How awful they must be to be kept separate like that.

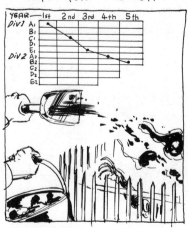

YEAR	1st	2nd	3rd	4th	5th
DIV 1 A₁					
B₁					
C₁					
D₁					
E₁					
DIV 2 A₂					
B₂					
C₂					
D₂					
E₂					

Halfway through year one, things are allowed to find their own level. It's 1c(1) for him, and from here you may trace the trajectory of Newton's apple: 2D(1), 3E(1). It sounds like the bidding in contract bridge.

"But, Dad if I had an outlet for my Art, it would improve my overall performance"

Beyond this point it's arguably no longer his own fault. They corral all the art students into one class.

"Which is the art class?"

"4A(2) but look, Dad, I promise I'll still play the violin."

With guys leaving into apprentice-ships, the bottom comes up to meet him. The art class is removed from the jostle of academic competion and set aside at the new bottom: 5B(2)

"Dad, they've gone and relegated the art class."

"NGGNNN!"

It a sad indication of the establishment's view of Art then, that it was a dodger's recourse, a view alas borne out by the scallywags inhabiting this class oh how he admired their scallywagginess.

But the real education was extra-curricular. The key is the free bus-pass. One of these gets you a week's ten rides, to school and home, on all city bus-routes. The trick is to get a spare one to use at lunch-times. Firstly, contrive to get your new issue without handing in the used one.

Next, avoid getting the last hole punched on Friday; jump off early, or hide from the conductor, or mooch a card off someone who's taking a sicky. Work it back along the card till you've got a whole free week. change the dates. It's basic prison-camp ingenuity

On the street where I lived - page 1

⑯

Starting a week with two blank cards, he'll be jumping on and off buses, tearing around the city with his accumulated lunch money, learning a million things; second-hand books, comics, Art gallery, the hunger for information outrunning the hunger for a ham sandwich.

The river, fish market, veg market, the starlings in George' Square, the damn peculiar smell trapped under the Argyll Street bridge in this whisky-bottling city.

And in the street where he lives, in his head, it's all on the same street, all the information, conceptualization and reek and one reminds him of the other.

Monet and Renoir are painting boats. Susan Sontag's telling passersby about "a vision of the world in terms of style"

In the Coffee-a-go-go, Lee and Kirby's Bernard the poet is reading his phone bill

While in the Silver Spoon, Gwen and Mary Jane are dancing to the juke box. How he wishes he could be in their world.

Marshall McLuhan's having a massage. Picasso's passing off another parsimonious cheque for his lunch, knowing it will never get cashed.

On the street where I lived. page 3.

Wee Eddie, since age 11, has the old '50s BATMAN ghost-artists down pat without knowing their names. "artist D" won't be "Lew Schwartz" for another 30 years.

He can't be snobby about Art after failing so triumphantly in order to get there.

Anthony! Come in for your tea!

CH no. 228.

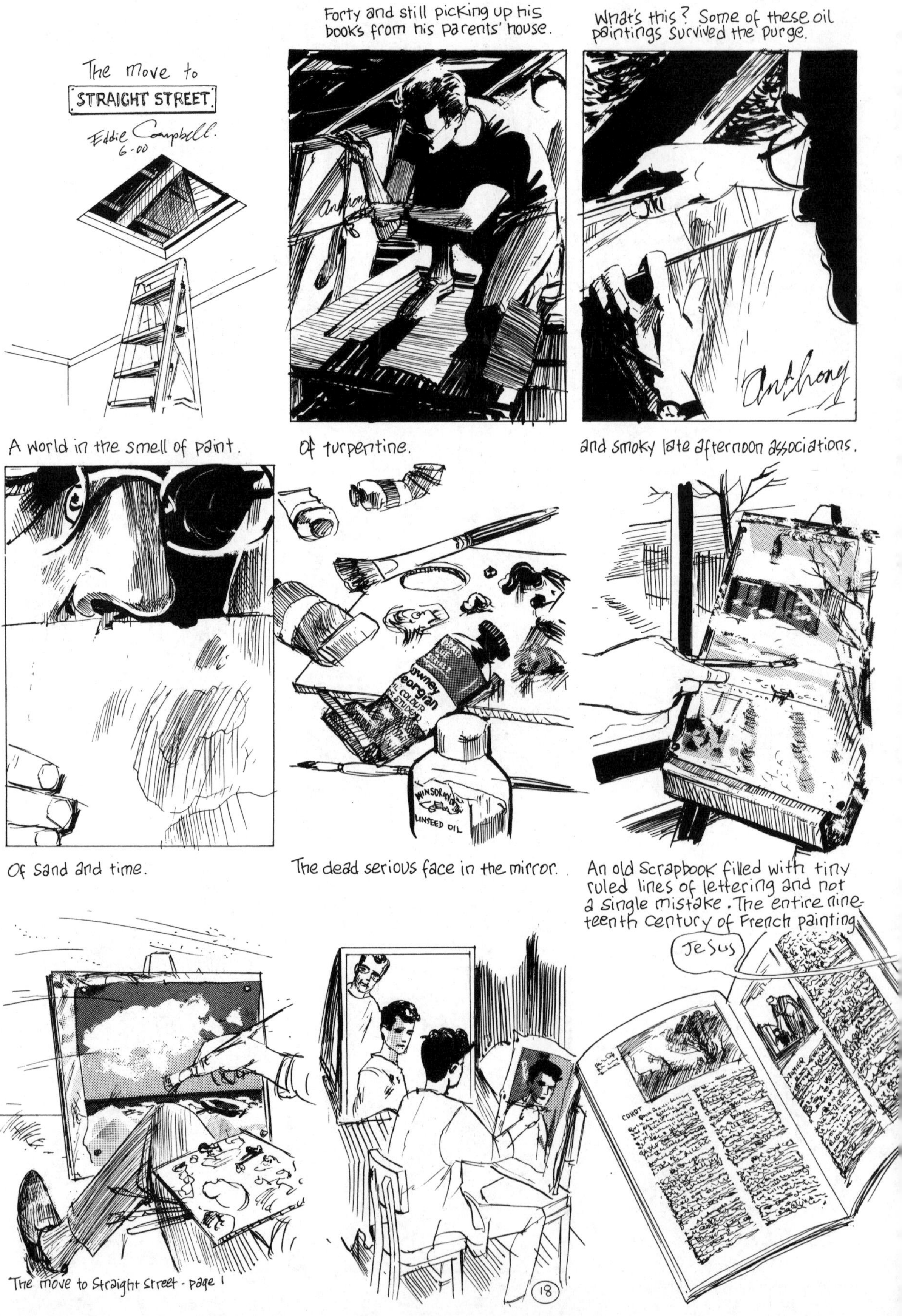
The move to
STRAIGHT STREET
Eddie Campbell. 6-00
Forty and still picking up his books from his parents' house.
What's this? Some of these oil paintings survived the purge.
Anthony
A world in the smell of paint.
Of turpentine.
and smoky late afternoon associations.
LINSEED OIL
Of sand and time.
The dead serious face in the mirror.
An old Scrapbook filled with tiny ruled lines of lettering and not a single mistake. The entire nineteenth century of French painting.
Jesus
The move to Straight Street - page 1

Then he had to move to Straight Street where the dreams get paved over.

Even wearing eyeglasses he can make no sense of the signs.

Get A-levels, get a career, get a driving license, 'get laid'.

Now he's got a girl friend. He meets her on the train when she's carrying an art portfolio.

He's feeling her bosoms in the park. He's coming in his trousers.

They're filling their time with daffy nonsense.

...in a fanciful shared place of the imagination that ends one day with a sulk.

He never knew why, just walked away.

Still, it was a mistake to make a pass at the sister on the way out.

The Move to Straight Street - Page 2

He's not sure how he got into art school after doing a joke picture for the exam.

He doesn't last long there anyway. what was he thinking? That he could make a living pouring the stuff in his head out onto paper.

Despite efforts by his supervisors to improve his standa: and the attention drawn to his shortcomings, Mr Campbell displays an apathetic lack of interest, his output is disappointing, there are too many omissions and his erro: rate is not acceptable.

Because of his general lethargy I cannot see that he i lik· ·   · ·mprove and can only report that I am not   ·the post of clerical ·

Another lot goes in the bin. All the comics with which he imagined he would astonish the world.

What a wanker! I'm going to punch him in the back of the head

No! You'll see it differently in a few years.

yes! He needs a wake-up call!

BOF!

URG

WHA—? Bastid!

It's a strange winter of the mind

where self-cancelled people notice each other on Straight Street.

It happens once in Paris. He's not sure if it's bad or good, a fight or what?

And he remembers that strange punch on the back of the head.

But which way to the Café Guerbois?

And what's he doing here anyway? and with all these condoms?

Why were you taking Sharon to Paris? I don't think you even like her. Her mother's been phoning here...

Mum! I'm not even in the door.

Monday morning. His heart sinks in the factory gloom.

And yet there's a calm here. A quiet respite. No pressure. Time to work things out.

Explain it to me. He had his chance at Art School, then he had a civil service job only an idiot could lose. What's the matter with him?

I'm worried.

Och, the boy's head's in the clouds.

SUNDAY TELEGRAPH

The Move to Straight Street - page 4

Eddie Campbell

Give us a hug then!

Eddie Campbell 6/99

There was a news item recently where Doctor Spock's son came out and said:

My father was supposed to be the expert in child rearing. His was THE book on the subject

It says it there see

But I'll tell you... he never once hugged us.

What a bunch of fuckin' pansies we have all become.

My daddy never hugged me and now I'm all fucked up

Boo hoo

You make me sick, the lot of you! You're a failure so you blame it on the old man? Give me a break!

My brother tried that one:

My therapist says it's all because you never hugged me.

But it's not too late to start.

Aw, so help ma boab.

Eddy, maybe it wouldn't hurt to give it a try

Och, a'm off to watch the fitbaw.

Give us a hug, then, page 1

DAD! I'm going back to London now

Oh alright. Come on, then.

There there

His dad certainly never hugged him. But men were tough in those days. In the trenches of France, Grandpa took a bullet.

His arm was all but useless thereafter, but he lugged a mailbag six mornings a week.

When I knew him he was retired and grandparents had big iron beds you could sit under.

A grouchy old guy except when he was checking off the horses

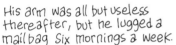

This is the sport of kings

He'd be perched there in front of the T.V. smoking his cigarette and licking the lead of his pencil. It amazed me that he never accidentally ate the wrong one.

Or he'd be at the piano playing one of the Seekers new hits, the only "pop" music he was prepared to accept.

Kings

He told you that, did he?!

— Now the carnival is over

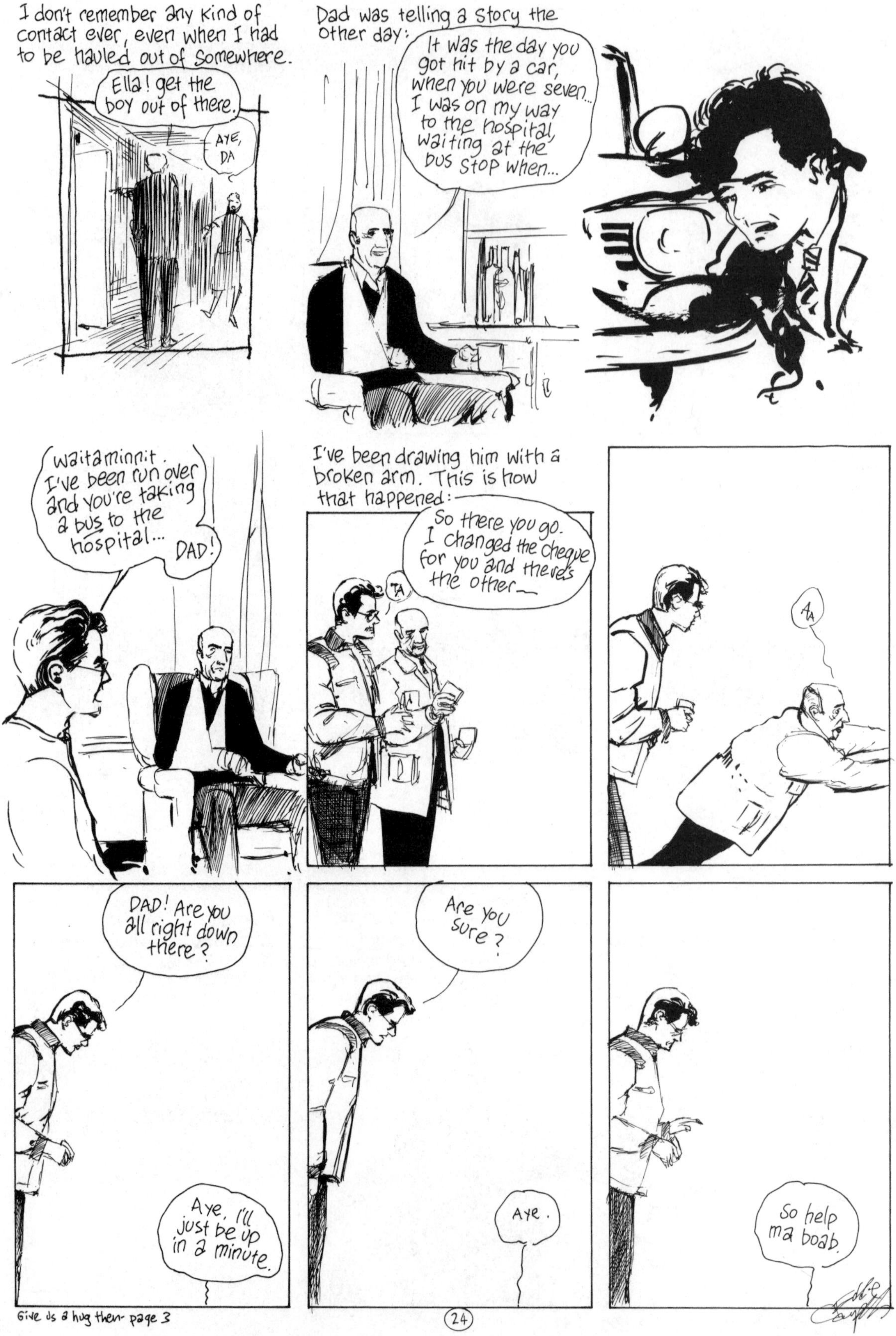
I don't remember any kind of contact ever, even when I had to be hauled out of somewhere.
Ella! get the boy out of there.
AYE, DA
Dad was telling a story the other day:
It was the day you got hit by a car, when you were seven... I was on my way to the hospital, waiting at the bus stop when...
waitaminnit. I've been run over and you're taking a bus to the hospital... DAD!
I've been drawing him with a broken arm. This is how that happened:
So there you go. I changed the cheque for you and there's the other—
TA
AA
DAD! Are you all right down there?
Aye, I'll just be up in a minute.
Are you sure?
Aye.
So help ma boab.

Give us a hug then- page 3

The Magus is house-proud

by Eddie Campbell.

30. 12. 98.

"I'm buying a house, Eddie. I have to come out of all this with something"

And of course, there is the basement.

ah! a basement...

So while we're in Britain we visit the Magus. He meets us at the Red Lion, with Melinda. A guy named Fred appears to be filling the role of chauffeur.

Fiery Fred is celebrated in the Magus' first novel, not published yet at the time of my visit. A man "...with the courage and fines of his convictions, both outstanding. He "was handling the door the night Iain Sinclair and... Brian Catling did their reading at the Holy Sepulchre"

Halfway through; an interruption. ("poetry hooligan.") Two teeth knocked out, blood everywhere.

The poets are gleeful at this real-life fracas. Read the book.

A lot of stuff has changed since I last saw the Magus only 3 years ago for a quick beer in London. I got held up that day because of a body on the tracks. His grim view of the world starts to get to you when you fall within his orbit. He's waiting down the line. You just have to get past a dead body.

I observe the changing cast of characters in his life as though they are the characters in his books, by the analysis of whom we may understand the authorial method.

Did *From Hell* open the door to a new reputation or vice versa. From Comic book guru to well known English oddball, requested for sometime TV appearances, once (an anecdote in the intro to one of the *Magus'* books) by Sinclair whom he notices characterized on the schedule as:

They pop up in each other's books. (Sinclair): "When we turned up (to photograph Christ Church) the building was filled with smoke"...

"A documentary was being shot in which Alan Moore realized the Church and its fellow East End Leviathans according to some dangerous occult prescription. (Christ Church) had willingly rented itself out as a set for Clive Barker's history of horror."

In his own recollection of the night, *I Keep Coming Back*, he's in the Ten Bells afterwards, a crucial site in *From Hell*. "I don't mean to do it. It just happens. Write about a place and you're cemented to it." Geographical locations become significant in his work.

In another pub, in his home town, he's painted on the ceiling in the company of 19th century poet John Clare. His grand subject narrows till it becomes this town; its presence, its history.

NOT PAINTED ON ANY CEILING EXCEPT IN HIS OWN HEAD

The Magus places the town of Northampton at the point in England furthest from any sea and characterizes it as "a black hole: "Nothing that gets out of here is not pulled back in""

An idealistic image from one of his earlier comics comes back to me: the Parliament of Trees: "Lived too long and grown too wise for the distractions of the world"...

"...so much that I had not imagined in the unmappable continent of their mind"

Perhaps our home town shapes us more than we'd like to think: Glasgow as a big river city with ships taking people somewhere else.

Each book takes the magus closer to home. The one we share is about London: "The pictorial aspect" (wrote Sinclair) "proved very seductive to the Hollywood dealmakers, who increasingly want product served neat."

The Magus - page 2.

Yes, Hollywood wants to turn *From Hell* into a movie. Somewhere, a green light is turned on.

He has an alchemical touch; not only the ability to create saleable ideas at the drop of a hat but also to turn the humdrum into something magical. This would be the magus' third foray into moviedom, but with not a scrap of celluloid to show for it.

A house, yes, with the rest of the money going out its windows in delicious clouds of fragrant smoke.

The magus has an idea to convert his house into a moorish palace.

Fancy glazed screens are installed, with order on one side and chaos encroaching upon the other.

The bathroom is developed under the enterprise of Fred, builder. He and his mates fashion the stainedglass porthole, depicting Asmoday, after a sketch made by the magus following his audience with the grand duke.

The magus sacrifices to his patron, the snake god, Glycon. Being a vegetarian, he burns only a cherished possession, a letter, a photo, its essence now removed to 'idea-space'.

Rats, some dozen cheery pets, live happily in his daughter's room in a bank of cages, free from any threat.

What do you think of all those rats then?

Dad, they weren't all rats! there were five rats, four mice, one hamster, a snake and a chombywomby.

chinchilla?

"The bed is comfortable and the big attic room serene, another Fred conversion."

As everyone knows, the joy of home ownership lies in being able to bang nails in the wall anytime you feel like it, without asking anyone's permission. One day the basement is dug out into an enormous dark cavern.

Anyone who has dabbled in renovations, or any creative endeavour for that matter, knows the difficulty of escorting one's original vision all the way through to a concrete reality.

It gets so far and has a tendency to stay like that. The magus turns to consider a delicate phrase for about four years or so.

"The smile might be mistaken for a friendly one..."

"...were it not for the cold, sardonic and unwavering superiority always apparent in Gull's eyes."

"To him, everyone else is a particularly amusing strain of paramecium."

Why, it seems like only yesterday that he converted his basement into the gaping maw of Hell.

Even if I get it finished, I'm here forever. I can never sell it...

Anybody who'd want a moorish palace wouldn't want it on Canal Street.

The Magus - page 4.

RUNNING A PUBLISHING HOUSE OUT OF THE FRONT ROOM

Eddie Campbell 7. 89
(+ Alan Moore script theft)

OLD
"HALF HOUR ECHOES STILL WHISPER AND CLATTER FAINTLY, A ZOMBIE SIBILANCE IN THE FAR CORNERS OF THE ROOM. MAYBE GULL EATS A GRAPE."

HE GAZES ABOUT AT THE VAULTED ARCHITECTURE AS HE WAITS, WHICH, ON BALANCE, IS PROBABLY MUCH BETTER FOR ONE THAN LISTENING TO "UP, UP, AND AWAY IN MY BEAUTIFUL BALLOON" FOR FIVE MINUTES."

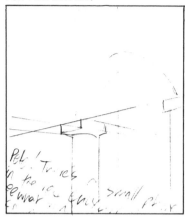

"AS THE TWO MEN STAND TALKING TO EACH OTHER, THEIR REFLECTIONS WAVER INDISTINCTLY IN THE POLISHED TILES AT THEIR FEET, THEIR VOICES RINGING IN THE STONE EARS OF THE DEAD PHARAOHS." shift to panel five.

"THE OFFICIAL STARTS TO GO UNDER * BEFORE THE AVALANCHE FORCE OF GULL'S PERSONALITY, ABOUT THEM THE DEAD LISTEN WITH VARIOUS ATTITUDES OF CELESTIAL INDIFFERENCE."

E FORCE OF
UT THEM THE
US ATTITUDES
L INDIFFERENCE
GLE NOW EDDIE
THE FOREGROUND,
O FACING AWAY
GHT ANGLE

what do you mean I "Could be anybody in the company."? It's NOT A COMPANY: I'm just running this out of the front room of the house

EDDIE CAMPBELL, of EDDIE CAMPBELL COMICS I JUST WANT YOU TO LEAVE OFF THE COMICS because it'll cost me eighty bucks to register the name for the purpose of a new bank account

RUNNING A PUBLISHING HOUSE - page 1

My, aren't we all busy little elves

Mick! Just in time for coffee.

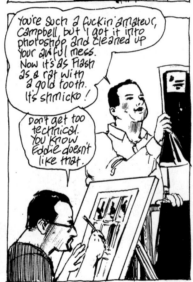

You're such a fuckin' amateur, Campbell, but I got it into photoshop and cleaned up your awful mess. Now it's as flash as a rat with a gold tooth. It's shmicko!

Don't get too technical. You know Eddie doesn't like that.

Now, I traded off some typesetting for the scans, but it'll cost us a carton of beer for the negs. 'mates rates!

I can't hang about here all day with you wankers

Wey hey!

Marcus!

Well look who's here

Just get your page here by Thursday.

You know the ad on the TV... the mint made for mouths. I've just had an idea.. what if they made mints for your arse?!

An arse-mint! brilliant.

Don't the Japanese already have them?

If you're not using it, that would fit nicely into the current Bacchus story.

I thought so too.

Why don't you put the kettle on.

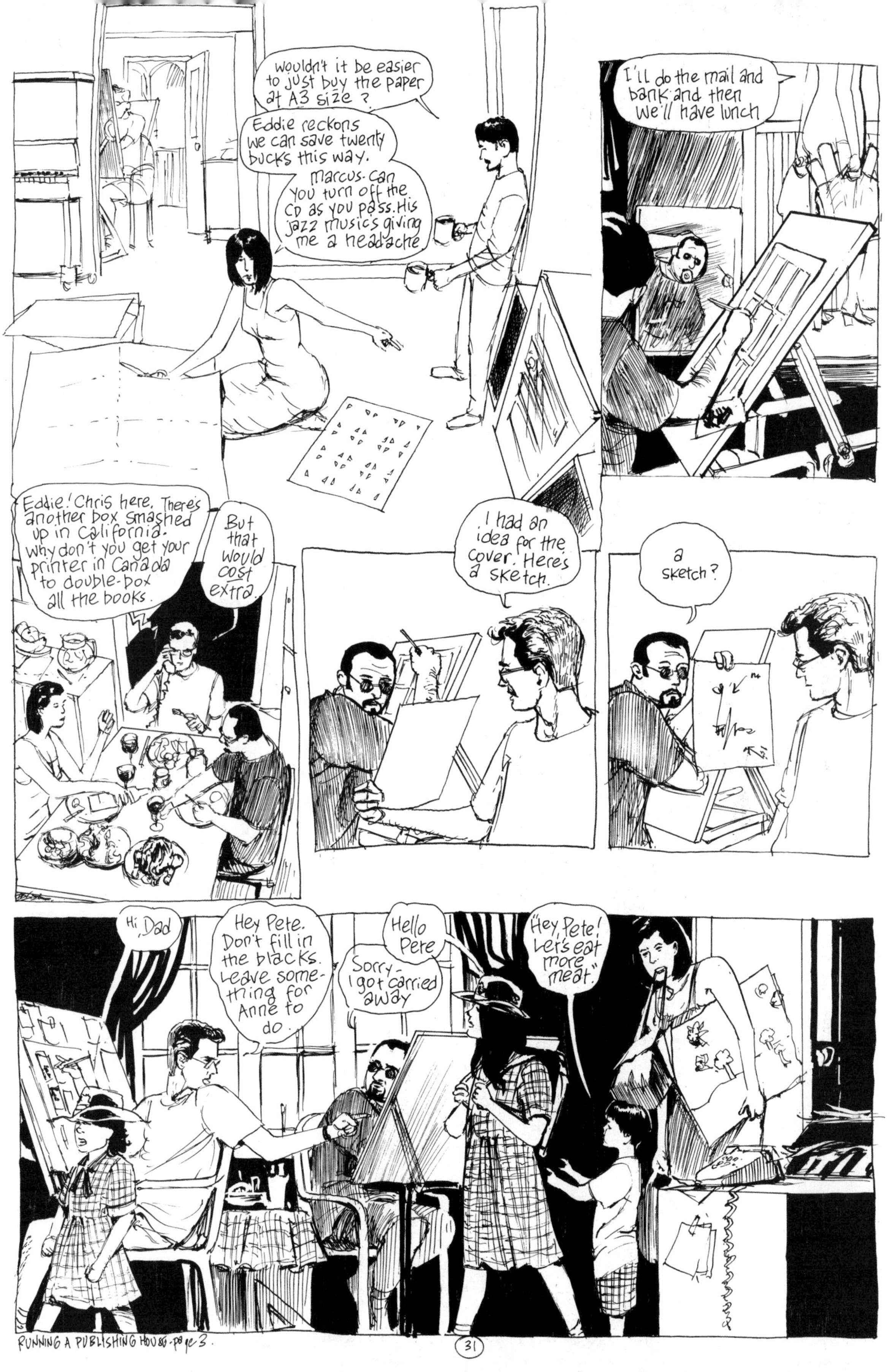
Wouldn't it be easier to just buy the paper at A3 size ?
Eddie reckons we can save twenty bucks this way.
Marcus. Can you turn off the CD as you pass. His jazz music's giving me a headache
I'll do the mail and bank and then we'll have lunch
Eddie! Chris here. There's another box smashed up in California. Why don't you get your printer in Canada to double-box all the books.
But that would cost extra.
I had an idea for the cover. Here's a sketch.
a sketch?
Hi, Dad
Hey Pete. Don't fill in the blacks. Leave something for Anne to do.
Hello Pete
Sorry. I got carried away
"Hey, Pete! Let's eat more meat"

RUNNING A PUBLISHING HOUSE - page 3.

Darl, I think you'd be more creative away from this chaos.

And then we could have the house back for living in

Here's the plan then: Mick and I will rent a unit. He'll live in his half and my half's the new studio.

Sounds good.

IT STARTS WELL ENOUGH →

Whisky at eleven in the morning? Well, I guess we should baptize the new studio.

Pete's wedding.

Pete's honeymoon.

Honey! I can't work here, I'm moving everything back into the front room.

cor, what's that supposed to be, Dad?

Eddie, this is Chalky. About that guy who wants cartoons for his new magazine. I saw him today...

Yeh, I told him h... ...h w ...anh don... think... likes it...

Nice painting, Pere. Dad should get you to do them all.

Why Thank you Hayley

Hey, Pete! Look at this cool thing I found.

Half a bloody hour it took just to bank a foreign cheque, so the xeroxes will have to wait till tomorrow

FED EX! You have a package for me?

FedEx
Federal Express

Oh, jeezis! I forgot about him.

What's Marcus doing asleep on the couch?

DAD! You said you'd take the fax out of my bedroom!

Eddie Campbell

Another sleepless night

Eddie Campbell
12-99.

...but then, of course, Herrmann scored Citizen Kane too

That would explain it.

PLEASE — WATCH OUT FOR CAT

I'll see you monday then

I might come on the bike if it's not too hot and I'm not too lazy

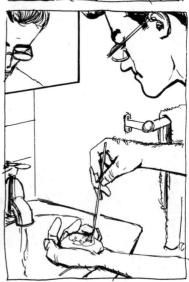

All-you-can-eat salad bar... or fish'n'chips?

FISH AND CHIPS

Puss

FISH LOVERS SUSHI

The cat with the broken miaow

Goodnight darling.

G'Night Daddy

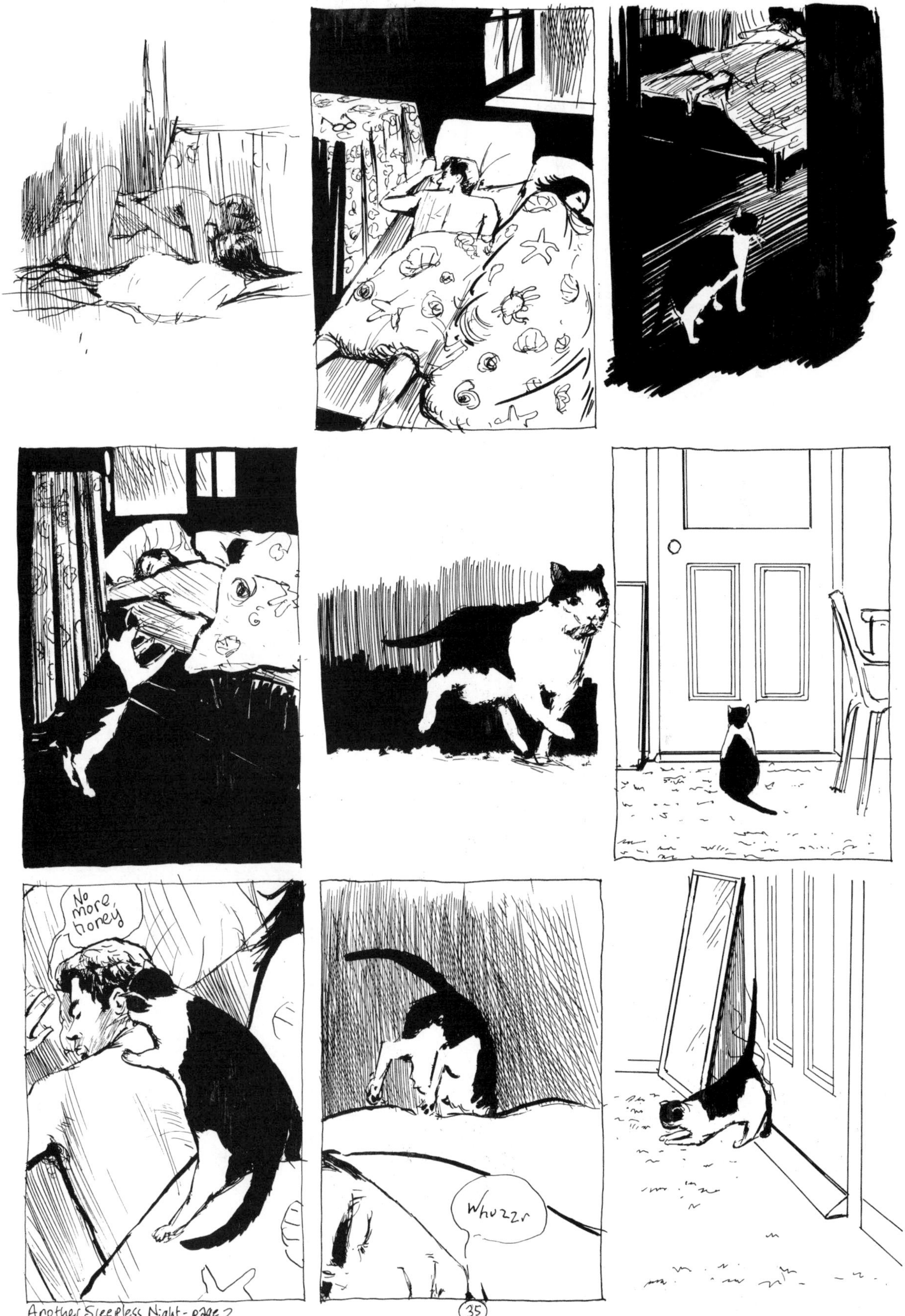
No more, honey
Whuzzr

Another Sleepless Night - page 2.

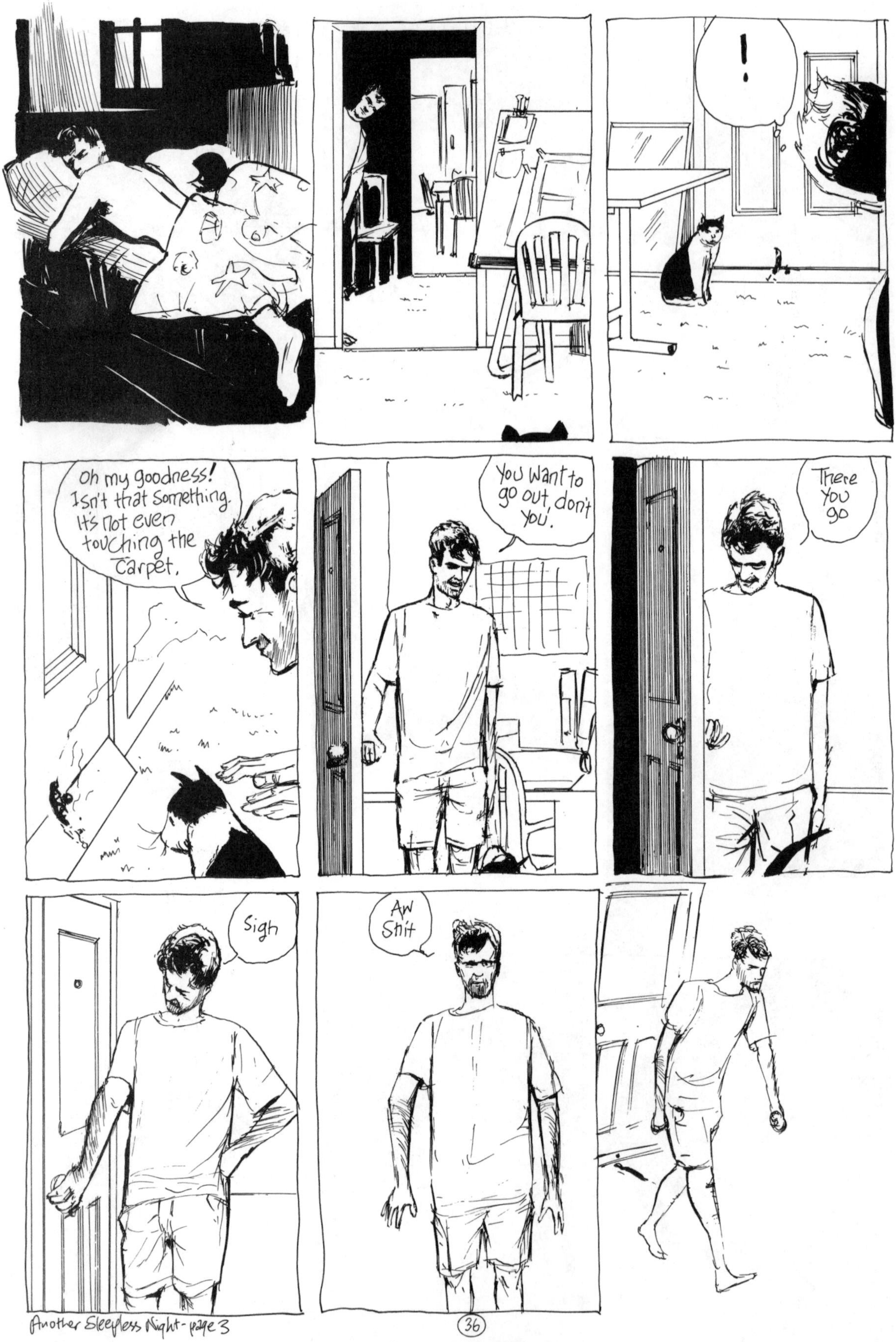
!
Oh my goodness! Isn't that something. It's not even touching the carpet.
You want to go out, don't you.
There you go
Sigh
Aw Shit

Another Sleepless Night - page 4

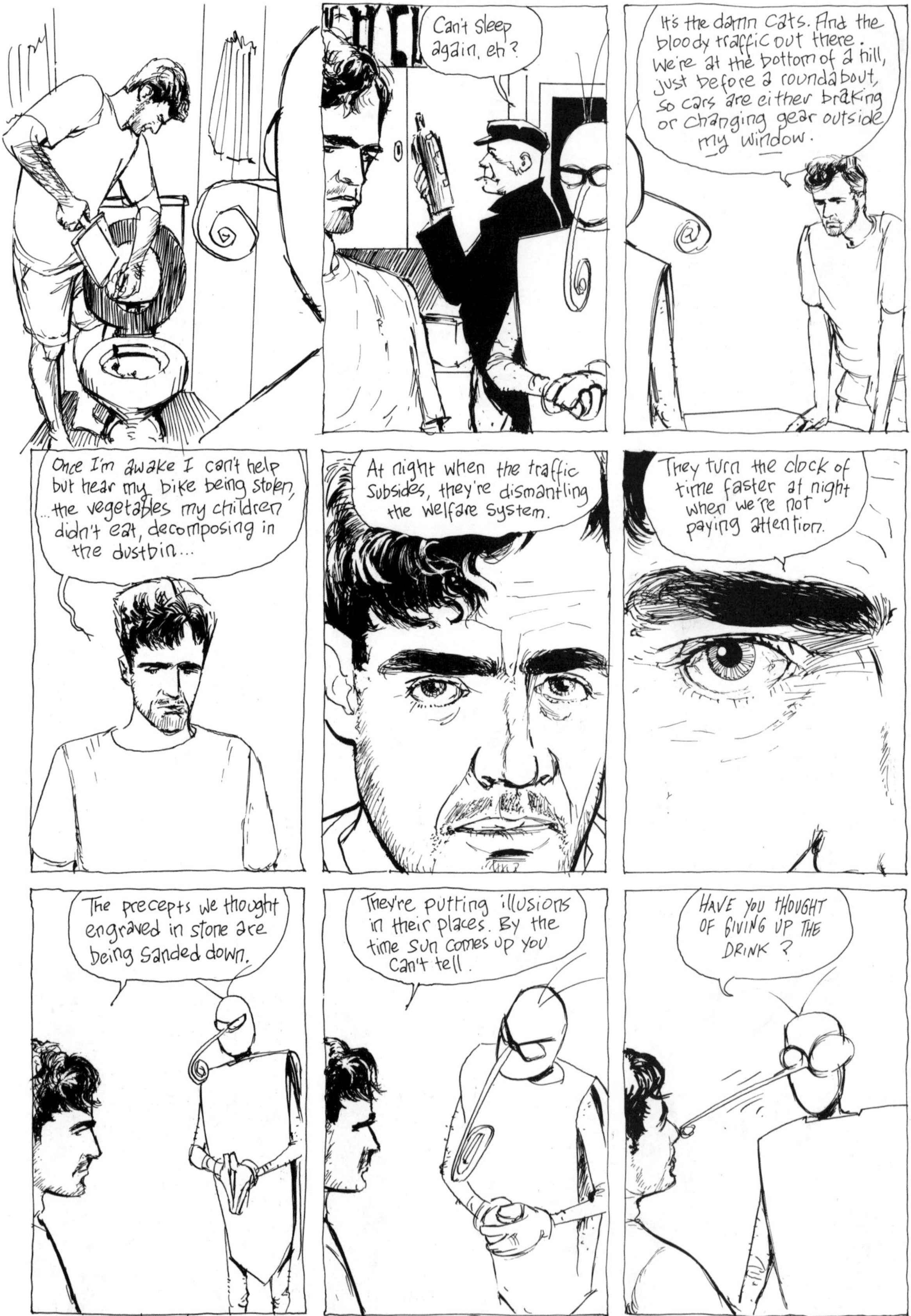
Can't sleep again, eh?
It's the damn cats. And the bloody traffic out there. We're at the bottom of a hill, just before a roundabout, so cars are either braking or changing gear outside my window.
Once I'm awake I can't help but hear my bike being stolen, ...the vegetables my children didn't eat, decomposing in the dustbin...
At night when the traffic subsides, they're dismantling the welfare system.
They turn the clock of time faster at night when we're not paying attention.
The precepts we thought engraved in stone are being sanded down.
They're putting illusions in their places. By the time sun comes up you can't tell.
HAVE YOU THOUGHT OF GIVING UP THE DRINK?

What has that got to do with it?

Drink has got to do with everything that goes wrong in you.

"Although moderate drinking will not kill irreplaceable brain cells, as once argued, alcohol use can interfere with sleep, with memory and with cognition.

How much would you have to pour down your gullet to qualify for that?

Well, how much do you drink?

I'm hardly a heavy drinker; a glass of white wine with my salad lunch, a gin and tonic in the late afternoon watching the sun go down from my verandah... a couple of glasses of wine with dinner...a wee nightcap with wifey while we review the events of our day...

SWOON

I shall start from the beginning.

A. Allergies: Alcohol is only one ingredient of alcoholic beverages. Others include grains, yeast, fruit, malt, molasses, spices, colouring agents and preservatives, all of which may produce allergic reactions in susceptible individuals.

B. Birth Defects: The Journal of the American Medical Association has reported: having just one or two drinks daily while pregnant is associated with a substantially increased risk of producing a growth-retarded infant.

C. Cancer: "After cigarettes, alcohol is probably one of the most important environmental influences on cancer." According to William Bennett of the Harvard Medical School Health Letter.

"Excess alcohol intake clearly raises the risk of developing cancer in the liver, mouth and esophagus. Many other cancers in the lung, pancreas, intestines, prostate and recently breast have also been related to alcohol."

D. Digestion: Alcohol irritates the stomach lining—

NO MORE! STOP!

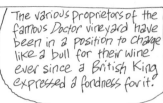

– the story behind this one?

Ah! The Doctor. The Elector of Trier, in 1360, seriously ill and fed up with his physicians, drank himself back to health. The vineyard was duly dubbed 'the doctor'.

The various proprietors of the famous *Doctor* vineyard have been in a position to charge like a bull for their wine ever since a British King expressed a fondness for it.

...while the neighbouring vineyards, it is said, have been justifiably miffed since their wine is just as good but sells for considerably less.

F.

Didn't think you'd fall for that old label hype.

I had to know for myself. We'd just got the down-payment for the movie rights.

We sped out in the car and spent 300 bucks on a handful of bottles of wine. It was a heady moment.

Look, darl! A furniture sale! We need a coffee table.

Stop the car. We'll shove one in the back.

And the other one you're holding; the *Colares*; a fellow in Portugal sent me that after I did the story about you and the vines curled up in bunches on the ground to keep them low out of the Atlantic winds.

Hi. Hypoglycemia...

He couldn't have known this ten year old red was vintaged in the year Annie and I got married. We drank it on our anniversary. It's so easy to forget that every empty bottle up here is a treasure. Only the special ones make it of course.

Each one was a place and a time captured in a bottle and another place and time in the glass. Almost every wine-making country in the world is represented here.

It was Julian Jeffs in his book about Sherry of Spain who wrote: "A man who drinks fine wine because he enjoys it will never become a drunkard. Wine stops being a pleasure long before it becomes a danger."

So many of you drinkards like to delude yourselves with this poetical nonsense. You cannot transcend the facts...

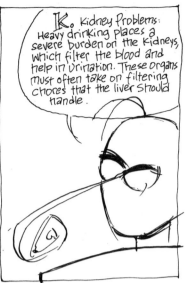

K. Kidney Problems: Heavy drinking places a severe burden on the kidneys, which filter the blood and help in urination. These organs must often take on filtering chores that the liver should handle.

L. Liver Disease: The most common liver disease is alcoholic hepatitis, or inflammation of the liver, which occurs most often in alcoholics but is also found in social drinkers. Cirrhosis of the liver is irreversible.

M. Menstruation. Alcohol is a ready but dangerous source of relief for women who experience the pains and depression of P.M.S. but many women do not realize that their physical tolerance for alcohol decreases sharply at this time.

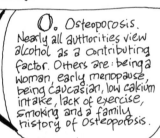

O. Osteoporosis. Nearly all authorities view alcohol as a contributing factor. Others are: being a woman, early menopause, being Caucasian, low calcium intake, lack of exercise, smoking and a family history of osteoporosis.

WHAT HAS ANY OF THIS GOT TO DO WITH ME?

My friend, we have arrived at the clincher.

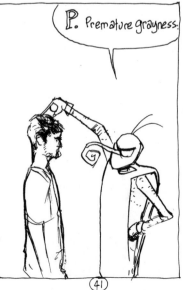

P. Premature grayness.

A drinkard who develops nutritional deficiencies is at risk for special hair problems such as diminished folic acid.

Wait a minute! A drinkard?

Take off the mask!

Ugnh

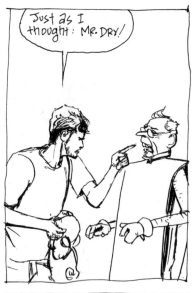

Just as I thought: Mr. DRY!

I wondered when you'd notice.

Of course! How could I be so stupid? *The Snooter* symbolizes the dark encroaching terrors of the night...

...while Mr. Dry represents that part of human society which presumes to know what is best for its fellows.

You are the Wowser; the Killjoy. You have no poetry in your soul and cannot recognise it in others.

My old pal Simpson used to recite a poem by Robert Herrick... lemme see if I can recall it... "Born was I to be old...

"And for to die here. After that, in the mould, Long for to lye here...

"But before that day comes,
Still I be bousing
For I know in the tombs
There's no Carousing."

You get yourself back to bed. I'll see this buzzard off the premises!

You want back in? Make up your mind.

CLICK

That means the Snooter is still out there... in the dark... Watching... waiting.

Bring on the morning! Roll all the demons up inside the curtains

A bright new day!

Daddy, if you gave food to your bottom, would it come out your mouth?

Of course it would, darling.

Another Sleepless Night - page 10.

43

Campbell

Eddie Campbell
3/00

VISITATION

"Look at them tracing their desperation, the makers of strong images.

Look at their ink clotting brown and black on the parchment skin

Look: they render us down there limb from limb,"

© Neil Gaiman
Angels and Visitations.

Neil Gaiman comes for a visit while he's down this side of the planet doing an appearance in Adelaide

It was a sci-fi con. A lovely lady named Helen organized my appearance and looked after me.

He came out of the same small-publishing milieu as I did, just after I left Britain and then he burst onto the international scene.

This would be the first time I'd really gotten together with him not counting a few brushes at convention parties (when the business still flourished enough for that sort of thing)...

...and a fragmentary communication I had with him on his answering machine when I was passing near Little Nutley and he still lived there.

Eddie, I was in the garden. If you phone again...

Determined to pin him down for a proper conversation, I've arranged to take up an open invite at the university to present a talk. This way, at least, we won't be interrupted

We omit to discuss the subject until the very last minute.

We'll just wing our way through the history of comics.

and I haven't really got the hang of talking on this scale yet, but it goes down well enough.

There are three things that distinguish the medium of comics. Thing one:

Actually, that's the opening of another speech on another occasion, but what the hey!

And they write us cheques there and then for $150 each.

visitation - page 1.

So I pick up some fine wines, we have dinner and everybody gets to meet Neil.

I've got two or three Australian wines here I want to tell you about.

Two or three?

Hayley's wearing Neil's famous jacket, a period piece which he reckons is made from buffalo or elephant hide or some other impenetrable beastie.

Chalky White's being belligerent about President Clinton's impending impeachment.

A politician's only skill is his good name and reputation. If he stuffs that up he's lost the reason he's there!

I'm not saying I vote for the guy, but if he does his job well enough, shouldn't we just be thankful and not make an issue of his private life?

At last we get some time alone.

No, it's not the drink, it's something about this phase of life, I think.

Or maybe it's just me. Things get easier, but it's all a veneer.

The Beasts of cancer and catastrophe lurk behind the phony curtain of daylight, with its cheery, gibbering distractions.

This is for you, Neil.

Visitation- page 2.

oh, this is wonderful. I can use this when I side with the dwarfs in the beleaguering of Angband.

And I will turn the tide of battle as I pick off the Balrogs, shooting them slap-bang upon their hairy bottoms.

But it's only a stick.

This "Stick"... shall have pride of place in my luggage.

Denis Kitchen asked me to write a Spirit story: I want you to draw it.

Will Eisner's SPIRIT! hoo hah!

I'll call you.

Darl, if money weren't a worry, what wine would you drink tonight?

eh? Money's always a worry. One of our distributors just went bankrupt.

We just had a party. Now it's back to work.

It's always either a feast or a famine with you

Visitation—page 3.

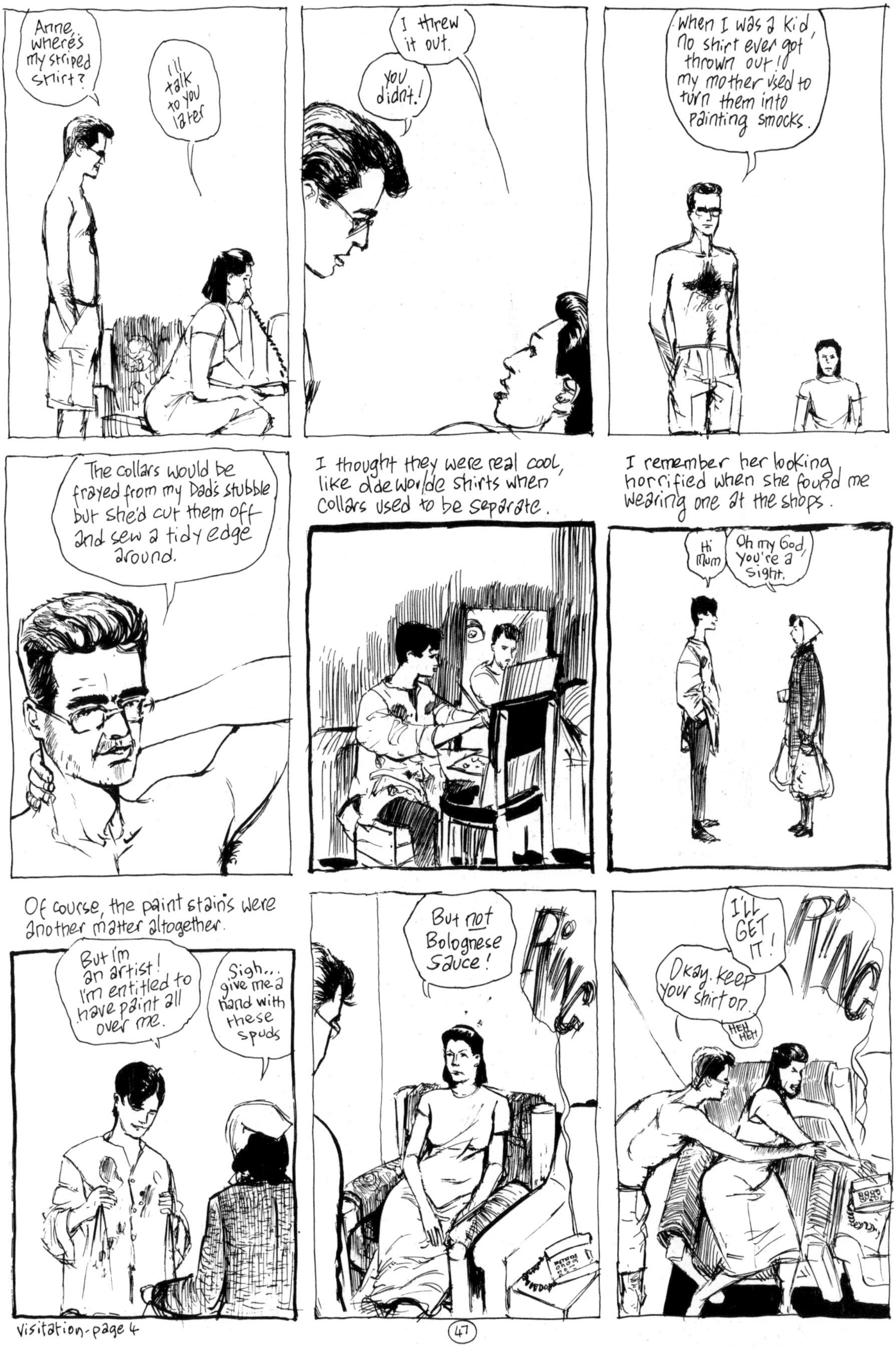

Anne, where's my striped shirt?
I'll talk to you later
I threw it out.
You didn't!
When I was a kid, no shirt ever got thrown out! My mother used to turn them into painting smocks.
The collars would be frayed from my Dad's stubble but she'd cut them off and sew a tidy edge around.
I thought they were real cool, like olde worlde shirts when collars used to be separate.
I remember her looking horrified when she found me wearing one at the shops.
Hi Mum
Oh my God, you're a sight.
Of course, the paint stains were another matter altogether.
But I'm an artist! I'm entitled to have paint all over me.
Sigh... give me a hand with these spuds
But not Bolognese Sauce!
RING
I'LL GET IT!
Okay. keep your shirt on.
HEH HEH
RING

Visitation-page 4

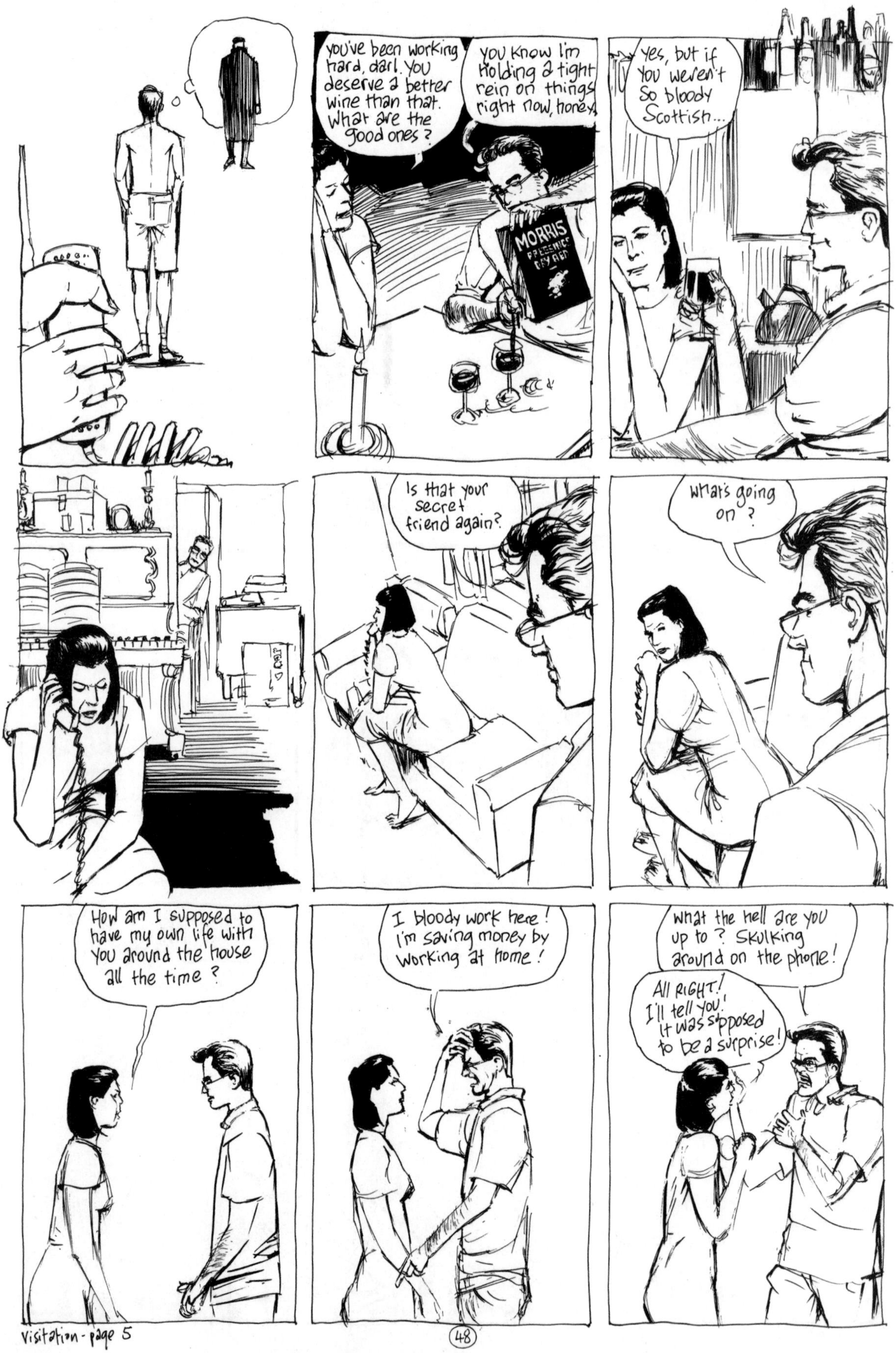
you've been working hard, darl. You deserve a better wine than that. What are the good ones?
You know I'm holding a tight rein on things right now, honey.
MORRIS
Yes, but if you weren't so bloody Scottish...
Is that your secret friend again?
What's going on?
How am I supposed to have my own life with you around the house all the time?
I bloody work here! I'm saving money by working at home!
What the hell are you up to? Skulking around on the phone!
ALL RIGHT! I'll tell you! It was supposed to be a surprise!

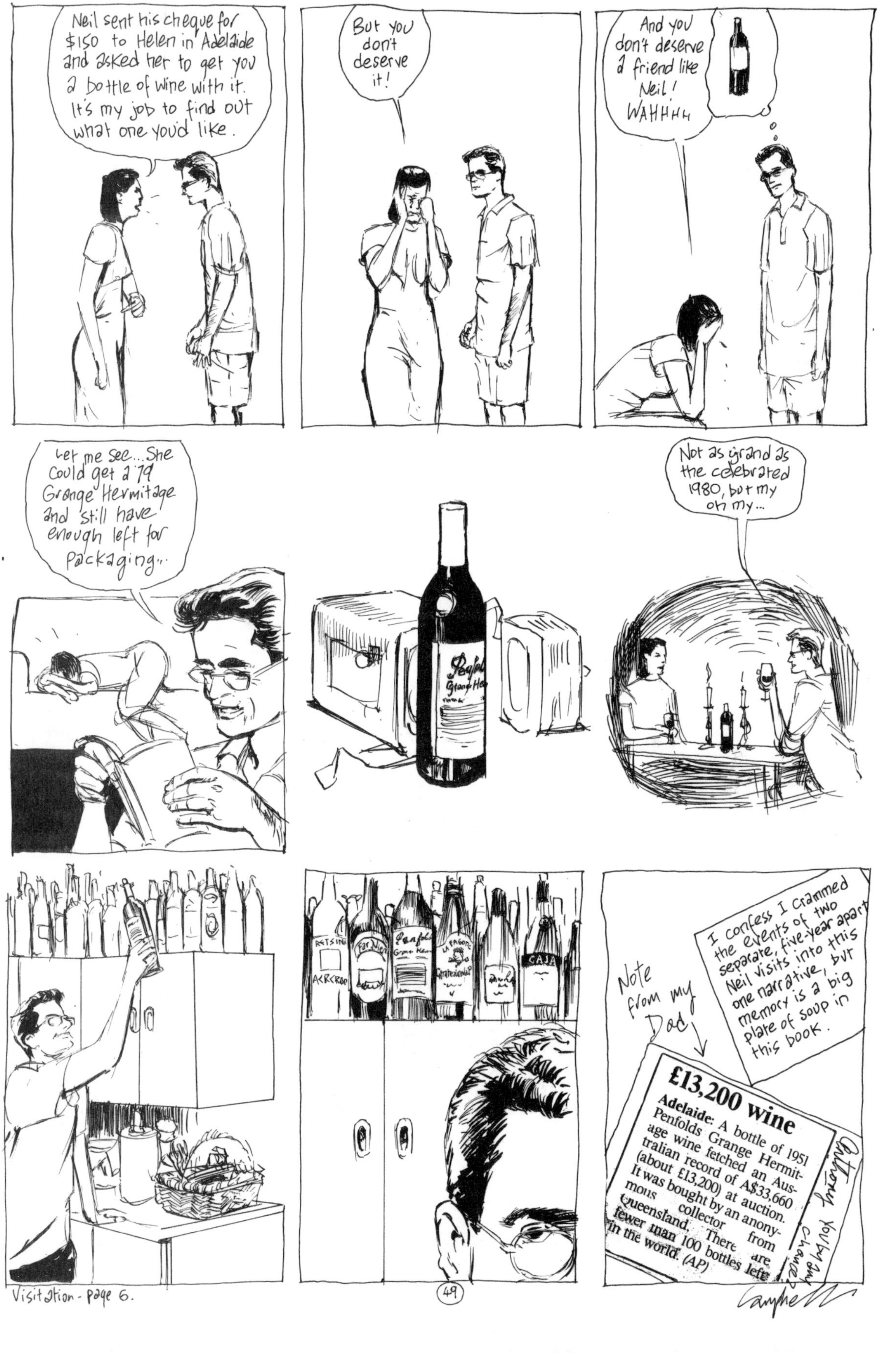
Neil sent his cheque for $150 to Helen in Adelaide and asked her to get you a bottle of wine with it. It's my job to find out what one you'd like.
But you don't deserve it!
And you don't deserve a friend like Neil! WAHHHH
Let me see... She could get a '79 Grange Hermitage and still have enough left for packaging...
Not as grand as the celebrated 1980, but my oh my...
I confess I crammed the events of two separate, five-year apart Neil visits into this one narrative, but memory is a big plate of soup in this book.
Note from my Dad
£13,200 wine
Adelaide: A bottle of 1951 Penfolds Grange Hermitage wine fetched an Australian record of A$33,660 (about £13,200) at auction. It was bought by an anonymous collector from Queensland. There are fewer than 100 bottles left in the world. (AP)

The acc⊙untant

CHALKY 1998 WHITE

Eddie Campbell 8.'00

"You can't drink that! It's your future."

It's quite simple, really. What you do is: set up an excluded superannuation fund, say the Bacchus Super Fund, with the Campbell family as the sole beneficiaries.

Then you buy an off the shelf Company and transfer a single share each to you and Anne.

You and Anne then appoint Yourselves as directors and as directors you agree to act as corporate trustee for the Bacchus Super fund.

You then make tax deductable contributions into the fund until you reach your specific age determined maximum, therefore considerably reducing your assessable income.

The contributions are taxed as they enter the Super Fund but that doesn't matter because, as a regulated Super Fund, tax is only payable at 15%.

Then, as corporate trustee, you determine that the investment strategy of the Bacchus Super Fund will be to invest in Fine Wine.

You spend all of the money on Grange Hermitage. You do a proper job and keep the wine cellared for ten to fifteen years and then sell it off at a considerable profit.

That's bloody brilliant! Okay, what do I have to do?

First you lodge form FD450-X74YF the bu... you m... wpla... b...

Babble babble

E Campbell

Football.

Eddie Campbell
7.99.

It's another photo hoax.

It's my turn to wash the Coca-Cola team jerseys. That means I've got them for the weekend.

Hey- we could round the gang up.

Yeah, that's what I was thinking. We could pretend to be a proper team and print the photo.

..white out the logos on the shirts of course...and I could paste it onto a shot of the crowd at Wembley. Can we get enough people?

We can always use the six-foot cardboard stand-up of Clark Kent out of the comic shop window.

Can he play soccer though?

Can't be any worse than Evans.

Fuck off and die.

We went by coach once to play a school whose name long ago disappeared into the fog of memory.

A fog no less dense than the one we played in that day. From the half-way line I can't see the straw-mop head of our goalie Pete Huddleston.

A pro match would have been cancelled in these conditions. Willie Callahan's rubbing his hands gleefully, glad to be out of the office. He's taken the day off work to see his boys in action.

Shuggy MacDonald comes out of the fog and goes back in; lapping waves and the horn of a coast-bound trawler.

Nobody knew him before he'd been brought in, a friend of a teacher's son, to shape this team, drilling it in the ways of intelligent team-play.

You can always tell complete amateurs by the way they all chase the ball around.

Yeh

Wankers

I DIDN'T HEAR that

Movement at the inside-left position. That'll be Jim Ireland. Looks more Jack the Ripper.

Now we're climbing up the league, game by game, and a bit of mist is nothing to us. Our home pitch is on a 15° slope.

Sound of Stephen Patterson thrashing about in the middle. Ball's coming FORWARD!

"Trust the instruments!" shouted Captain Biggles.

"Everybody will be where they're supposed to be when you come out of the clouds, flying low."

I skim it across to the right. yup. Wee John Murphy's got it.

What's happening over there? Is he dribbling it around in circles again? Oh! It's back!

It's up to me! It's all noise and my heart's in my throat. The goal's in front of me!

I'm in slow motion. I'm halfway toward it.

Now I'm half of that distance.

To regular eyes I'm not moving, like the wee man on top of the trophy.

If I went back to that pitch today I'd still be on it, frozen in time forever. Prehistoric ice-boy.

You're always taking pictures of yourselves you never take any of us girls

Yes, but this is a jest on a collossal scale

Wear the jumper, Callum. You're supposed to be the ball boy

No!

I've brought some funny hats

I brought my netball trophies like you asked. I hope you're not going to break them.

Where's Slattery? He said he'd be here.

OUCH!

by

Eddie Campbell
2000

i didn't know i'd been hit by the car, although later I could recall everything up to the point of launching myself off the pavement.

i came to on the staff room sofa looking up at all these adults who were uncharacteristically concerned about how I was feeling.

this is creepy, my head being in the warm place where their bottoms usually sit.

then there's the peculiar swirly view of the world I get from the stretcher.

You'll be fine, son.

that awful antiseptic smell that engulfs me as they carry me into the Victoria Infirmary

Aw, the poor wee lad

From my window I can see the lights of Hampden Park. Dad was going to take me to the International match tonight.

HEY! BACK TO BED YOU.

when he gets here, I suggest we can still do it, but it's no go. there's a conspiracy and the grownups are all in on it.

what a bummer.
at least I've got my pyjamas now in case anybody sees me.

next morning the old guy in the next bed has gone home.

they put a boy in there who's a little older than me.

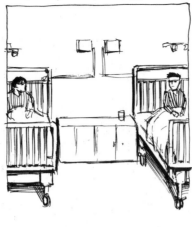

a nurse hands out some comics. i get a Beano. The other boy is given some strange and a wonderful looking thing, all in colour. what can it possibly be?

i'm crestfallen. why was he thus favoured? i lie in a stew of hatred.

when he's asleep i steal a look

my goodness.

who's the guy with the patch?

© MARVEL COMICS 1965

and more important, who is Stan? Who is Jack? I guess these are all drawings. why didn't that occur to me before?

what a magic otherworldly quality, but with all the cheeribliness of this one, also the tragicness, trans- posed whole to the other.

if only i could take it home. but such a treasure would surely be missed. they would come to get it back.

where do you find these? the local newsagent's got a rack. i always thought i wasn't allowed to look at these

my goodness. nobody stopped me from buying it.

here's another newsagent. now. why are these all different issues from the other shop? i can start to piece together narratives where the missing portions are even more special than the ones i have.

Strange, obscure shops which i imagine will be unchanged
So many years from now, in spite of the closed and condemned one with a Green Lantern in the window with only the blue not yet faded

it's a mystery. No two shops ever get the same selection. i know they're not always old ones that have been lying around for months because I get to open the bundles at one place

it doesn't really occur to me that there should be a system. i half believe that they deliberately print them in such a higglety pigglety order.

except that the letters pages are mailed from a happy land where you don't have to even wait till January to get the January issues, let alone look for them all over town.

i'm travelling further and further afield, in great secrecy. Oh no! i forgot to ding the bell and i've missed my stop. i'll be late home. i'll be found out.

Ouch! page 3

i must risk a jump.

ouch!

oh my goodness!!

hell's bells! i'm going to have to wear my bag back to front from now on, and hide it in my room.

At least Marvel Collectors' Item Classics didn't get wrecked.

One day i try to draw like Jack.

Now that you can draw comics yourself, you won't need to buy them any more.

Eh?

How dare you! the men who draw these don't breathe the same air as you and me.

the comics still bear the smells of the happy land far far away.

i'm not sure which is the more magical, the incredible hulk and the fantastic four, nick fury, or Stan, Jack, Steranko, Will Eisner

SPECTACULAR CHANGE EVER RECORDED, AS HE ONCE AGAIN BECOMES-- THE HULK!

STORY AND ART BY MARVEL'S MODERN MASTERS: STAN LEE and JACK KIRBY

INKING: MICKEY DEMEO LETTERING: ARTIE SIMEK

i squint my eyes and look into one of those dimensions you get in comics where maybe Stan and Jack are just Mr. Lee and mr. Kirby like ordinary adults

and not nearly as famous as the beatles.

go and buy a 'masterworks' volume, so they don't string me up for using the pictures
Eddie.

The Fan

Wee Eddie Campbell.
1998

Meeting your heroes is always daunting.

"Oh, my God! It's really him."

At the San Diego Comic Convention I'm on a panel with Will Eisner where the subject is: Comics about real life. It would be 1989 or '90

It's Sunday Morning. Not too many people have got out of bed to hear comic artists seriously talking about real life.

came all the way from Poughkeepsie to ask a question.

Kim Thompson

Klingons

hasn't been to bed yet

This guy's always at the front.

After, I tell Will who I am.

"You must send me your book"

"You bet."

Inevitably, it all looks different when I get home.

"Ah, Will's too busy. He doesn't want to be bothered reading my silly little book."

I never send it.

But Sometimes after a few beers I picture Will at home in Florida...

...after these past eight years, going down to his mail box...

"Still no book from Eddie."

Campbell

Imagining the Creative Life

Wee Eddie Campbell
9. 00.

What did I imagine being an artist would be like, when I imagined it?

An artist? Yes, but you be a commercial artist if you want to make a living.

A what?

I'd never met a real artist. There weren't any on Straight Street, as far as I know.

There was a lady neighbour who had a book published about her experience in the Nazi death camps, titled 'Selected to Live' but that wasn't a career thing.

I'd never met a cowboy either but I never saw that as an impediment to becoming one.

Hello, Anthony

Have you got any sweets for me?

Each of us tells our our own personal life story to ourselves every day.

I should have done it differently

I'll never get over that

BEAT THAT!

Someone observed that the problem with television is not that it fills the child's head with nonsense but that it robs the child of the time to take itself away into a corner and narrate its own story to itself.

POLICE BOX

today Anthony saved the world fom the DALEKS

Eddie Campbell, the conquering artist.

Claude Monet said that to paint a picture you must first see it in your head.

DAMN!

Let's say that it works the same way with a "life".

Get a life, Eddie

OKAY

A Life

Off the peg, sir, or to measure?

I could think of no reason why I wasn't already a real artist except that the real business of art would appear to consist of fighting to establish a new idea in the world.

An Idea!

Oh, for an idea!

The heroic myth of the conquering artist.

You'll do

i'm next

ACME NOVELTY

When Art narrates its own story it tells itself that it is dead.

Pop Art blew a raspberry at my funeral.

The idea of Art as a continuum goes out the window.

It's absurd to still think of Art that way

How can you say that? there will always be Art

The picture in my head goes too.

You're an educated bloke. Why do you do this job?

I don't know

It took years to replace it with another picture of the creative life.

Ah yes, the creative life.

Now, let me see... we'll move everything from column A to here. Then if I revise the way I do the bookkeeping...

...so that spare cash shows up earlier over here... hmm... Ah yes! - the illusion of wealth. I'm a magician!

Then, by the day of reckoning, invoice 405 should come in...

But 407 arriving early would be a safer bet.

I'M HO-OME, DARL.

Oh shit

working hard?

Yes, darling.

SKETCH SKETCH

The Creative Life

Eddie Campbell
JAN 96.

The Creative Life - ·/96 - page 1

...who steals in at night and nibbles whatever provender is left lying about.

...who shits and pisses on healthy stores.

You owe me an accounting, and while you're counting you may count me...

...your enemy. Eddie Campbell

File that for re-use!

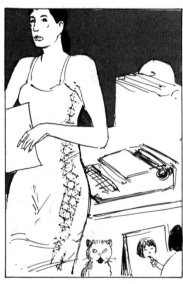

EDDIE CAMPBELL'S BACCHUS

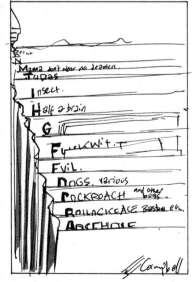

Mama don't wear no draewers.
Judas
Insect.
Half a brain
G
Fuckwit.t
Evil.
Dogs, various
Cockroach and other bugs
Bollackeace Bastard etc.
Arsehole

Campbell

The Creative Life - page 2.

Used car dealers
are human too.

Eddie Campbell "89

John, another hypothetical: a friend of mine signed a contract to buy a car... hmm yep... yes, ... hum. Okay given all that... how many legs does he have to stand on: a) Two b) one c) less than one.

Tell your friend he's fucked. These car people get out of bed earlier than you... I mean your friend.

Jesus suffering fuck.

ZZZ.

Right then! I have girt my loins for battle.

You've got your plan of attack all worked out.

yup

Now, regarding the automobile which I have purchased...

I have been a silly boy and I would like you to let me off lightly here. You have my deposit. I'd like you to keep that and permit me to renege on the rest of our agreement.

I see, Mr. Campbell. This is most irregular. Do you feel that we have coerced or otherwise imposed upon you?

Good heavens, no. I have only myself to blame.

sigh.

BIG SALE

Mr. Campbell, we like the gentlemanly way you have gone about this, and we want to give you your deposit back.

Why, thank you, sir.

CHEERS

MOTORS

Used Car Dealer - part 2.

The Chair.

You made it up, Campbell. This never happened.

My fellow artist from up on the hill saw us throwing out a broken chair and asked if he might have it.

Up on the hill he repaired it by nailing a plank to its underside.

The plank stuck out a foot and a half on one side, a fault he intended correct as soon as he could borrow a saw.

No saw in Campbell's tool-box, as you see.

But, upon consideration, he found that it made a useful support for his cup of tea.

And also for his TV remote.

And his book and his reading glasses.

Up on the hill, the extended chairbase has become all the rage.

Eddie.

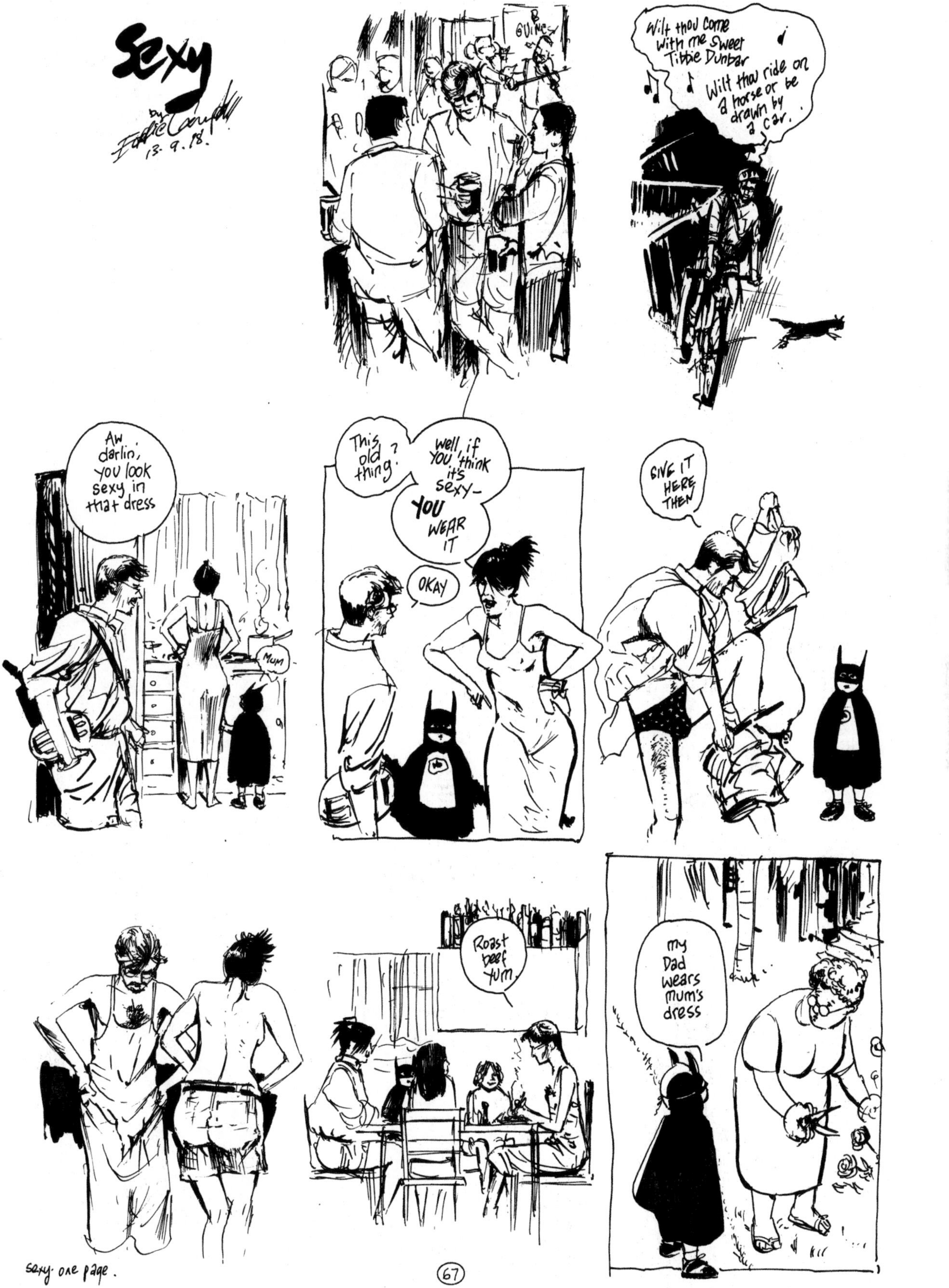
Sexy
by Eddie Campbell
13.9.98.
Wilt thou come with me sweet Tibbie Dunbar
Wilt thou ride on a horse or be drawn by a car.
Aw darlin, you look sexy in that dress
Mum
This old thing?
Well, if you think it's sexy–
YOU WEAR IT
OKAY
GIVE IT HERE THEN
Roast beef yum
my Dad wears mum's dress
sexy. one page.

grooming yocky's arse

Eddie Campbell
7. 99.

Sometimes cats are apt to chew the lawn for medicinal purposes known best to themselves.

One day Yocky's having trouble sitting down. His bum is giving him a spot of bother.

Upon examination, Annie observes that he has a leaf of grass sticking out of his arsehole.

A good two inches of blue cooch.

After giving it an investigative tug...

She trims it for him with her manicure scissors.

She performs this delicate grooming for the next two days until the problem works itself out.

how embarrassing.

PETS

by Eddie Campbell
9-00.

Puss was found out in the country by our next door neighbour, left to fend for herself with her brother.

She decided to jump the fence and live with us instead. We named her by committee.

Merlot

No, Puss

Puss

Ps

Sox came from across the road. He also got renamed by the lowest common denominator.

Mummy, why won't our cat live with us any more?

Yocks!

Rosie was a lost peach-faced lovebird that landed in our patch and was being menaced by Puss.

WOUNDED →

We bought a cage to keep her safe. One day she got out.

Tweet!

Then we got a pair of lovebirds to put in the cage and named them Bill and Coo. One did a flyer and the other got birdie-cancer in its wing and was put down.

exeunt

Dad, why don't we catch him up there and put him in the empty cage

Aw leave him be. He's happy

Yeh, but he's not doing anything.

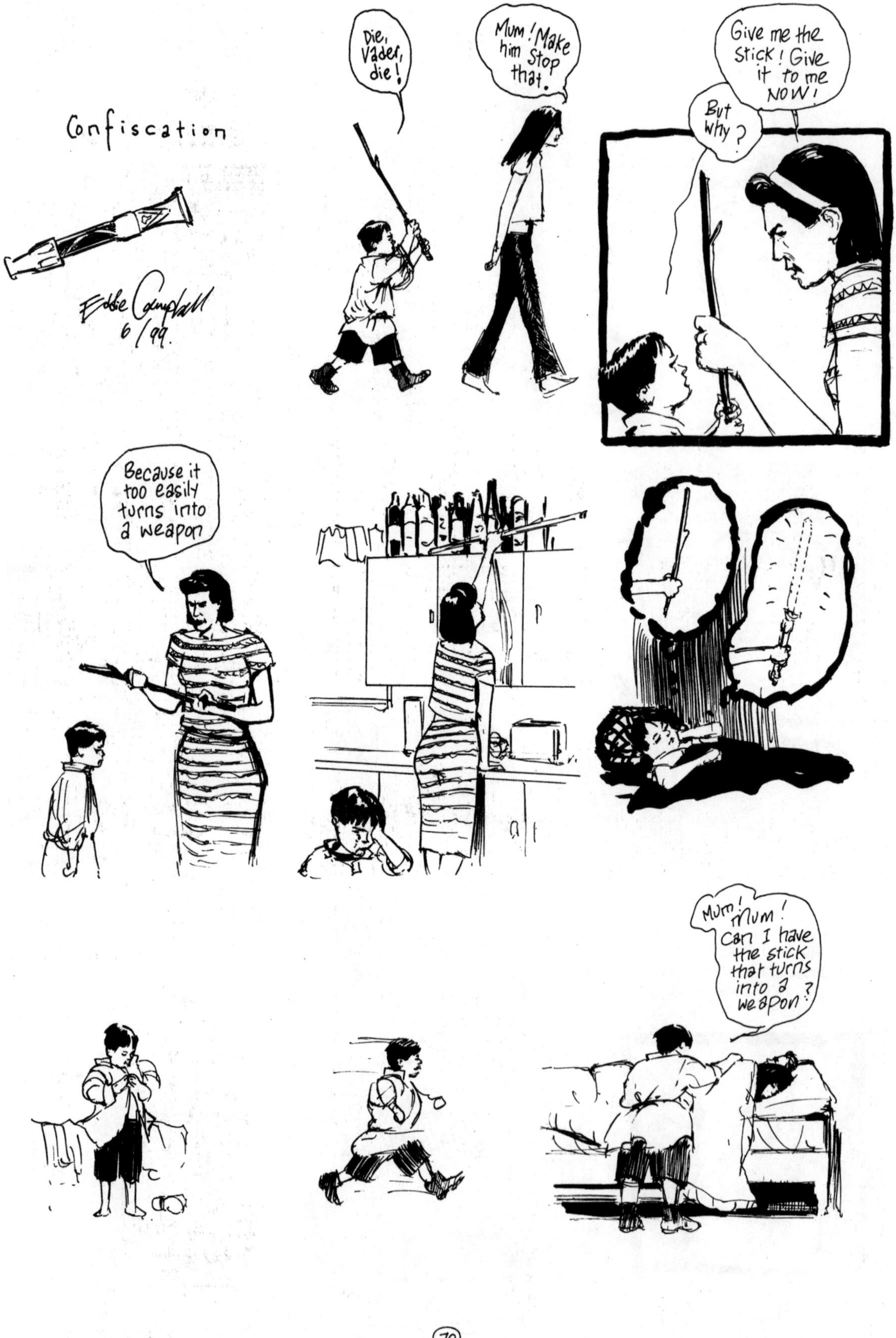
Confiscation
Eddie Campbell 6/99.
Die, Vader, die!
Mum! Make him stop that.
Give me the stick! Give it to me NOW!
But why?
Because it too easily turns into a weapon
Mum! Mum! Can I have the stick that turns into a weapon?

WALLYHOOD
Eddie Campbell
10/98

Will I be changed by "success"? Will it go to my big stupid head?

It's the story of Jack the Ripper. I'm not sure why they needed to buy any movie rights since it's a much retold historical event and the chances of the details of our version not getting changed around must surely be slim.

I think the bookkeeping has to show that an idea, or property, has been purchased otherwise the investors might think nothings doing and somebody's pulling a fast one.

It's the *Information Age* and our graphic novel is an access route to the information. Who'd have thought all that time rummaging in Victorian detritus would pay off? The movie deal started at Disney/Touchstone but they wanted a happy ending.

Then New Line had it while Sean Connery was eagerly sought for the role of the copper. Somebody else has got it now. This is all normal.

There must be a lot of people out there making good livings from not making movies. Myself, I just got paid my share of another year's option money. Thirty thousand bucks in my account.

Now I'm worried about the amount of tax they're going to amputate, with the end of the financial year only two weeks away.

We could get a computer— there's a nice deduction.

I donno...we've managed without one up till now.

I'm sure you'll think of something

Wallyhood, page 1

wallyhood. page 2.

(Doyle spot-illo, punch c.1849)

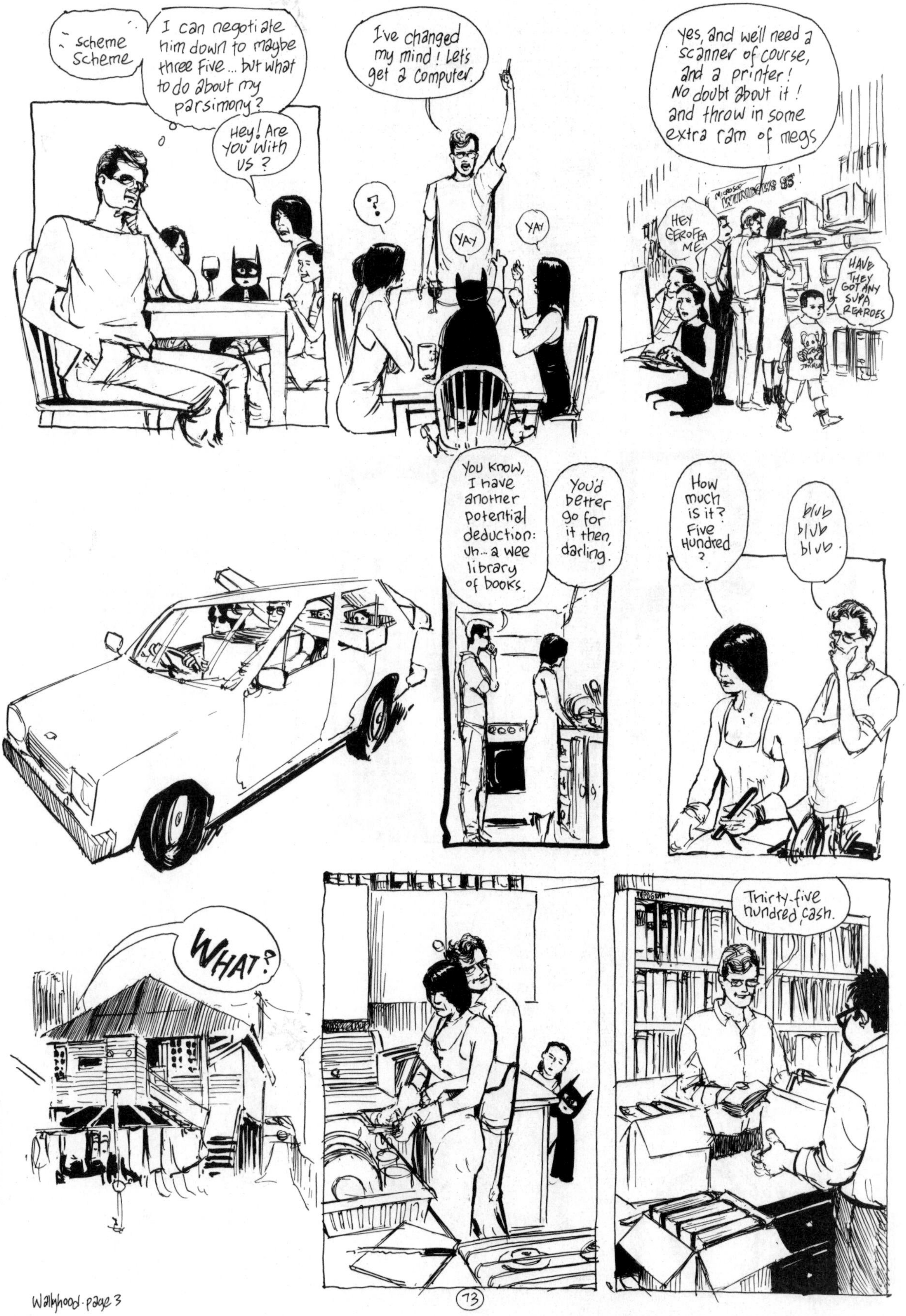
scheme
Scheme
I can negotiate him down to maybe three Five ... but what to do about my parsimony?
Hey! Are you with us?
I've changed my mind! Let's get a computer.
?
YAY
YAY
Yes, and we'll need a scanner of course, and a printer! No doubt about it! and throw in some extra ram of megs
WINDOWS 95
HEY GEROFFA ME
HAVE THEY GOT ANY SUPA REAROES
You know, I have another potential deduction: uh... a wee library of books.
You'd better go for it then, darling.
How much is it? Five Hundred?
blub blub blub.
WHAT?
Thirty-five hundred, cash.

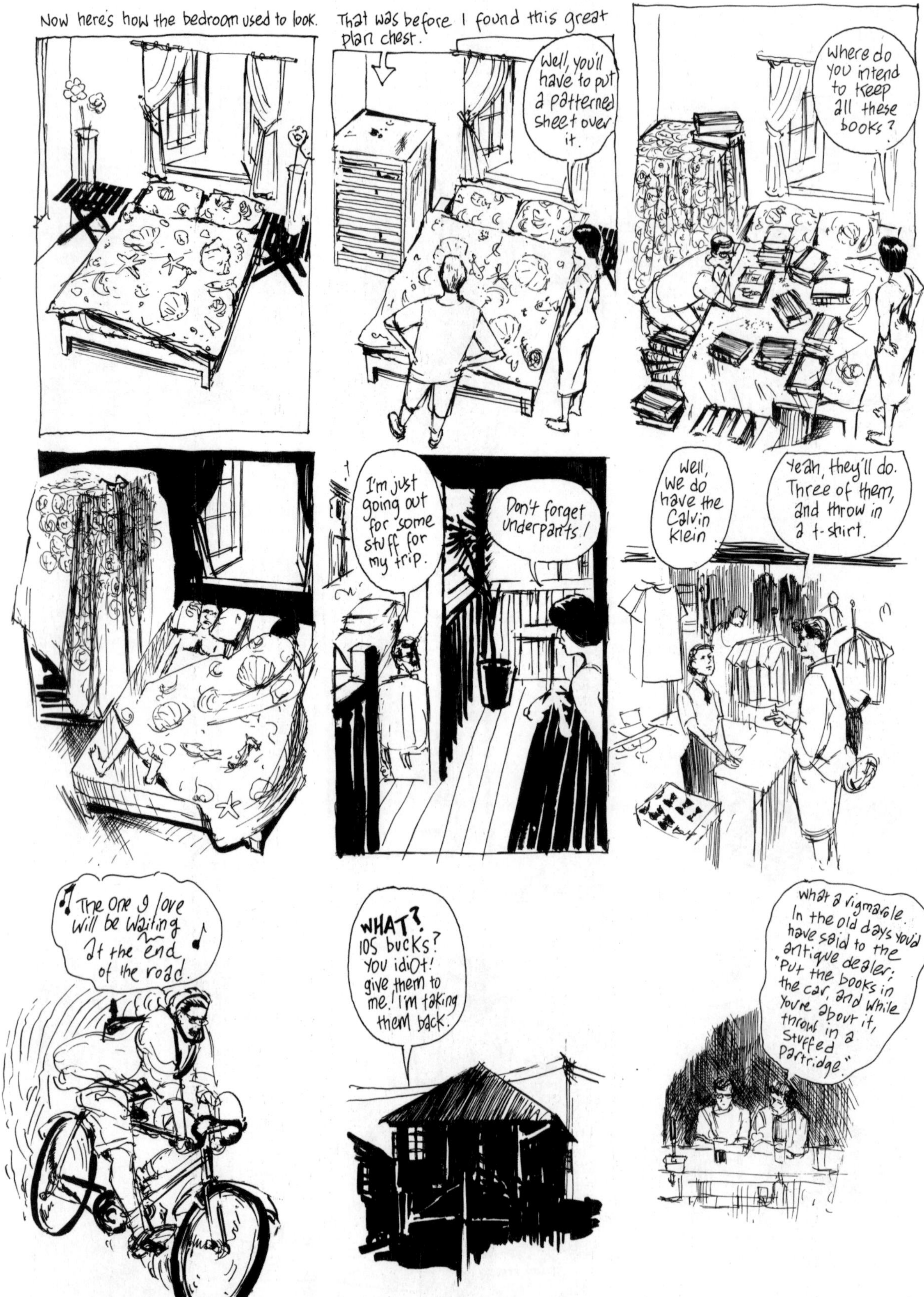
Now here's how the bedroom used to look.
That was before I found this great plan chest.
Well, you'll have to put a patterned sheet over it.
Where do you intend to keep all these books?
I'm just going out for some stuff for my trip.
Don't forget underpants!
Well, we do have the Calvin Klein
Yeah, they'll do. Three of them, and throw in a t-shirt.
The one I love will be waiting at the end of the road.
WHAT? 105 bucks? You idiot! give them to me! I'm taking them back.
What a rigmarole. In the old days you'd have said to the antique dealer: "Put the books in the car, and while you're about it, throw in a stuffed partridge."

wallyhood page 4

The Court Sketcher

Eddie Campbell 3/18.

How did I get into court-sketching for the T.V. News? It was Mullins.

Pete's been working with me since I got the idea about eight years ago of running my show along the lines of an old fashioned workshop.

Are you staring at me?

Just tell me, what's that written on your forehead?

How's that going to get us anywhere?

Look, I'll show you.

So I'd have an assistant or two doing backgrounds and stuff and Annie running the "office", supplying cut paper, cleaning and dispatching finished art, putting on lunch, etc., with everybody paid by the hour.

This was just ahead of my start in self-publishing. Pete Mullins grew out of it after three or four years but still puts in an occasional day for the social value.

His main gig these days is with Channel 7 News, freelancing the animated weather charts and other odd-job stuff like sketching at the trials.

Now there's something I wouldn't mind trying at least once in my life.

I've always found it an attractive concept, that of the artist as journalist. It's honest and down-to-earth.

It's a job that all but disappeared with the nineteenth century when they figured out an economic way of printing photos.

The man on the spot would do his sketch, then get it back to the art-room in a finished state to be hand-engraved on wood by a craftsman working to a tight deadline. A big picture would be sawn into smaller blocks which would be worked on simultaneously by a team and then bolted back together. You can usually see the joins if you look.

(Winslow Homer covers the Civil War for Harper's. He also sketched in court at least once but clearly didn't enjoy it)

Court sketching is the last outpost of illustrated journalism, if only because there's a prohibition against cameras at trials.

Plane crashes used to be recreated for print on the artist's drawing board. Now it's done on the computer for tv. News. Mullins and team reconstructed a tidal wave disaster at Papua New Guinea that went national.

This guy obviously didn't leave the office for this.

● Telegraph artist PAUL LENNON'S impression of the jumbo jet collis
At least 550 died in the worst crash in c
mbo jets collided in the Canary Islands tod
ARED KILLED ON
RY ISLANDS RUN

He was undervalued then, as now, the artist out there, producing to order and doing it fast. In a word, Professionalism.

Professional. Now that's something I've never been called.

Campbell, you're a complete fuckin amateur.

Don't get Campbell. He's not a team player.

Mullins is a true pro. He can turn his hand to almost anything, which is why everybody wants him all at once.

EDDIE, Channel 7 lent my pics to Channel 10 last week and now they both want me but I've gotta wrap up this spread for PICTURE magazine.

Thus it is that he calls me to fill in for him.

Can you handle Channel 10 and I'll juggle the other two.

No worries

That's how it started. Pete gave my number to Channel 10 and I got in there and enjoyed it, though I'm sure that in the heyday of this kind of work this was a gig you did early in your career when you were working your way up out of anonymity

So how come there are not a hundred upstarts vying for it? Maybe they've spent too much time at the computer and neglected the figure drawing.

So I'll be in the cafeteria working my observations up into full colour while Sharon Marshall tapes the report in one of her colour-coordinated jackets.

ten

RED

It gets me out of the house and into the mainstream of life for perhaps a couple of mornings in a month. And my God, there's heaps going on out there. Here's the blackguard who abducted a boy for sex.

Here's the prison breakout team

This pair set fire to a vagrant

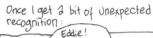

This bloke shot his wife because he thought she was having an affair.

Unnerving the jury by writing down their names during the selection process.

This girl survived a double suicide and had to carry the can for her more successful boyfriend. The judge dealt with her very sensitively.

Once I get a bit of unexpected recognition:

Eddie! I saw you do a talk once at Ozcon!

I'm looking forward to the FROM HELL collection

Another time I find myself sitting next to Mullins. It's like we've just moved the whole studio up to the Supreme Court, borrowing each others' pencils and all.

Pete had sat in the empty jury box for a good angle on the accused. I presumed he had permission and joined him. Then they moved us. Very embarrassing.

And being on the TV news is kind of cool because everybody knows about it. They think I'm suddenly getting somewhere even though publishing a monthly comic is significantly more complicated and also more lucrative.

I'm taking it all in my stride. But that first time I was pretty nervous. Soon as I got the call, I showered and shaved, ironed some trousers.

I rounded up pencils, erasers, pen, correction white, Pantone colour markers, several sheets of paper, backing card for when I hand over the work ... extra flesh-tint pencils ... uh, a scalpel to sharpen them ... removable magic tape.. lightweight drawing board..

Met up with Sharon and got some clues as to what was needed.

There's a possibility the only witness won't talk, in which case the trial would be aborted and we won't have much time.

GREEN

The security is intense. My tools are sifted and checked: my pencils, my erasers, my correction white, my paper, my markers, my board, my tape. The scalpel is removed and I am called to explain it.

Inside, I am greeted with a formidable scene. Four villains in a big iron riveted cage with bulletproof glass. They stabbed another jail inmate 53 times. The blood ran from wall to wall. One of them has got something tattooed on his forehead.

I envision my presentation: the big solid cage with its rigid lines; the prisoners contained like dangerous animals.

I lay out my tools; pencils, colour pencils, erasers, markers, pen, correction white, paper, card, board, tape...

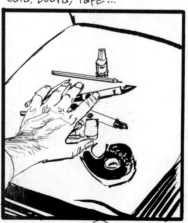

I have neglected to bring a ruler. I have two hours, starting from now...

Metamorphosis

12.00

Eddie Campbell

For the benefit of the jury...

Please describe the events in their precise sequence

I was sitting by my open window contemplating the annoying complacency of people...

I need a symbolic form, by which to strike fear into their hearts.

That's it... I shall become a hideous insect of the sleepless humid night.

I shall remind them of their childhood terrors... of snakes under the bed and beast droolings in the dark that make you afraid to put your bare foot on the floor.

I set about my transformation that very night.

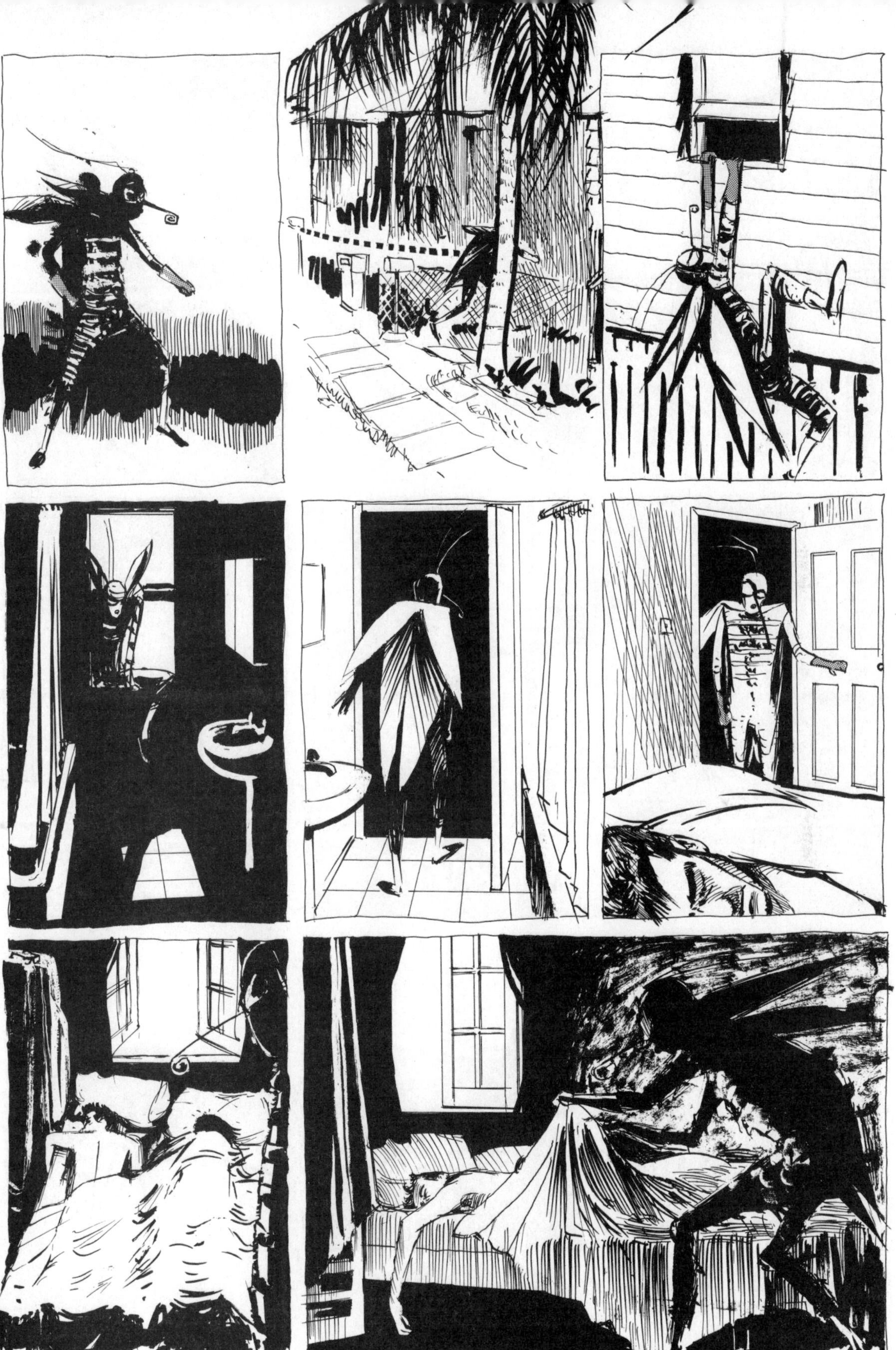

Metamorphosis - page 3

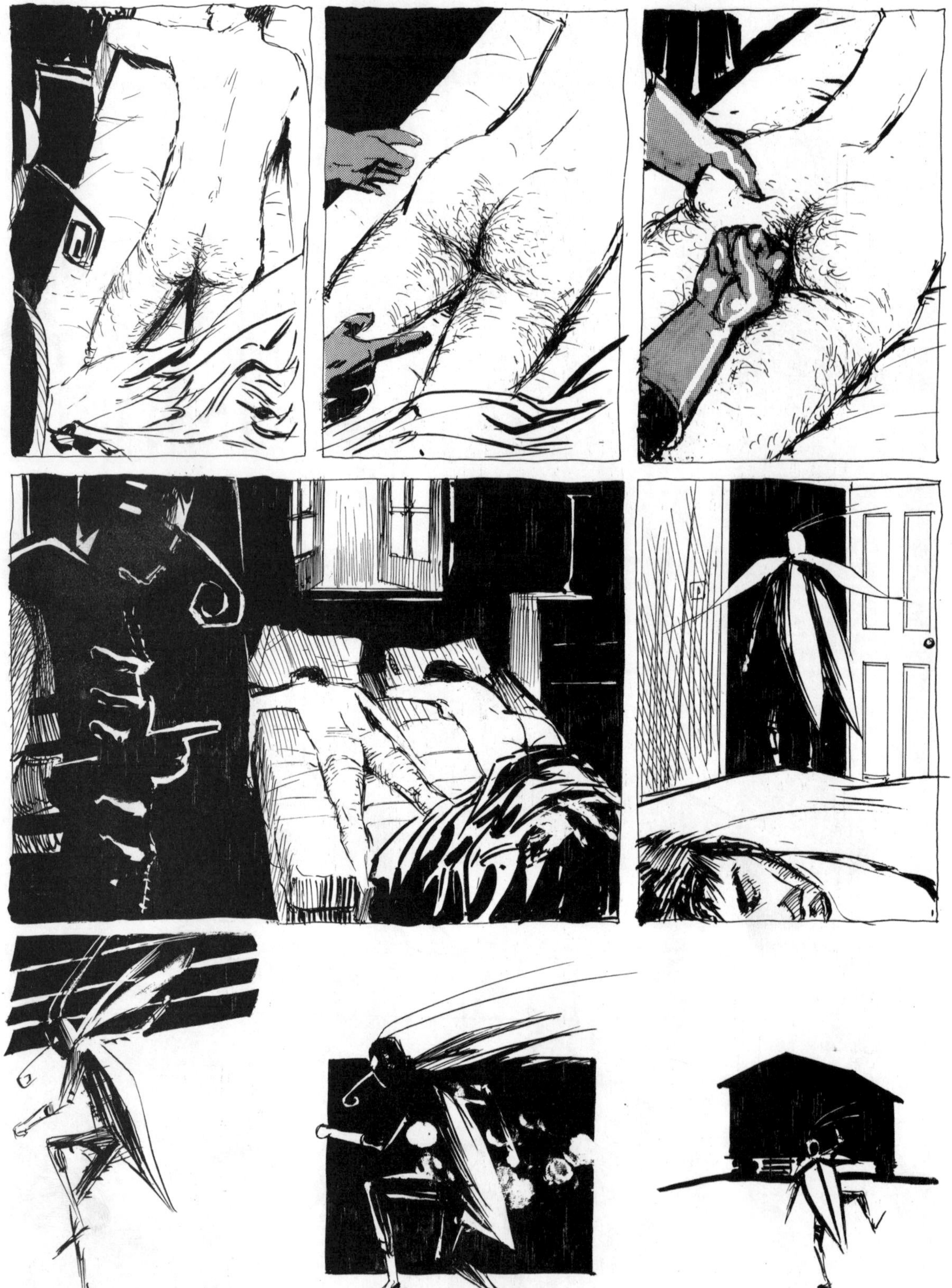

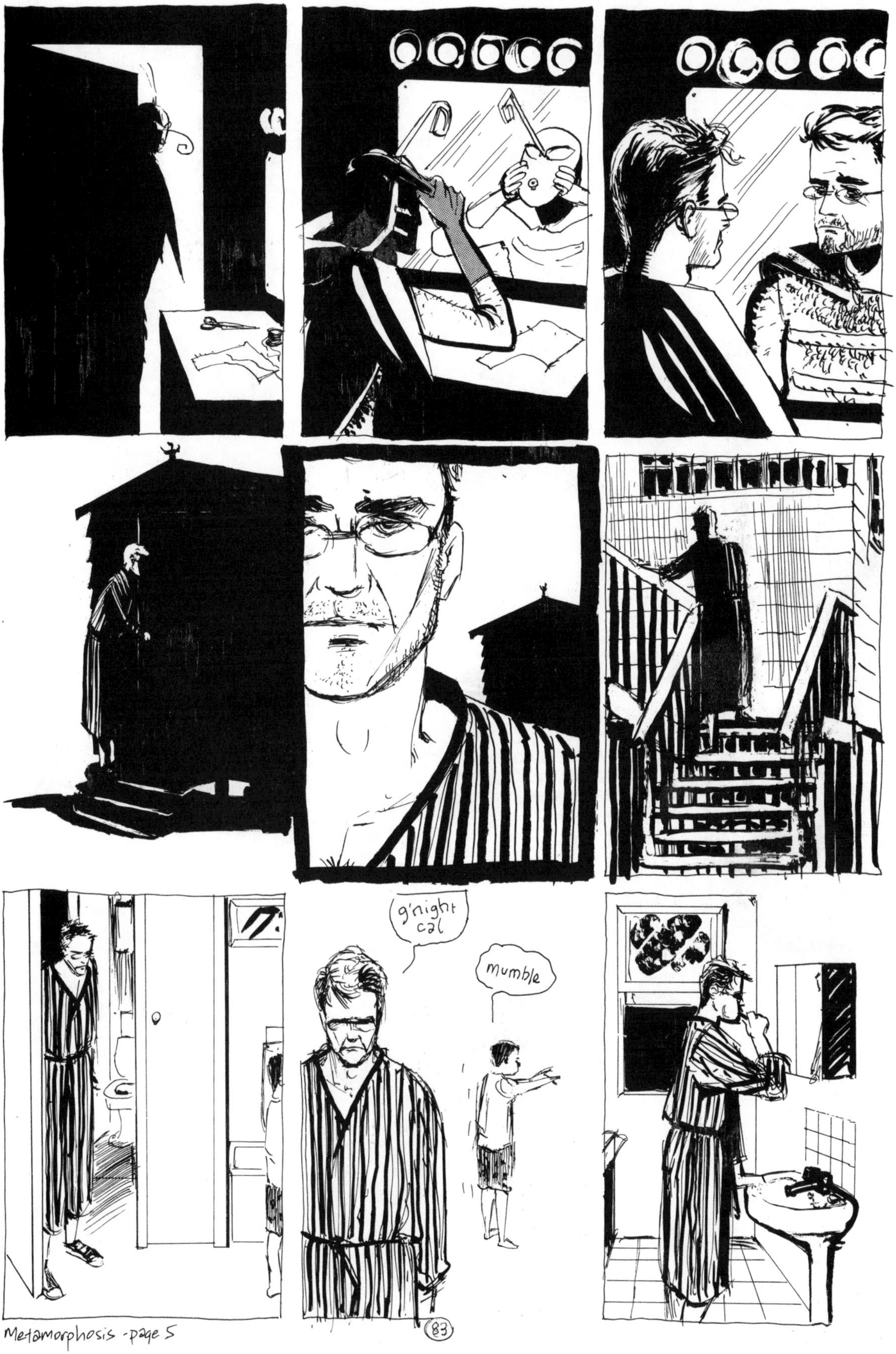
g'night cal
mumble

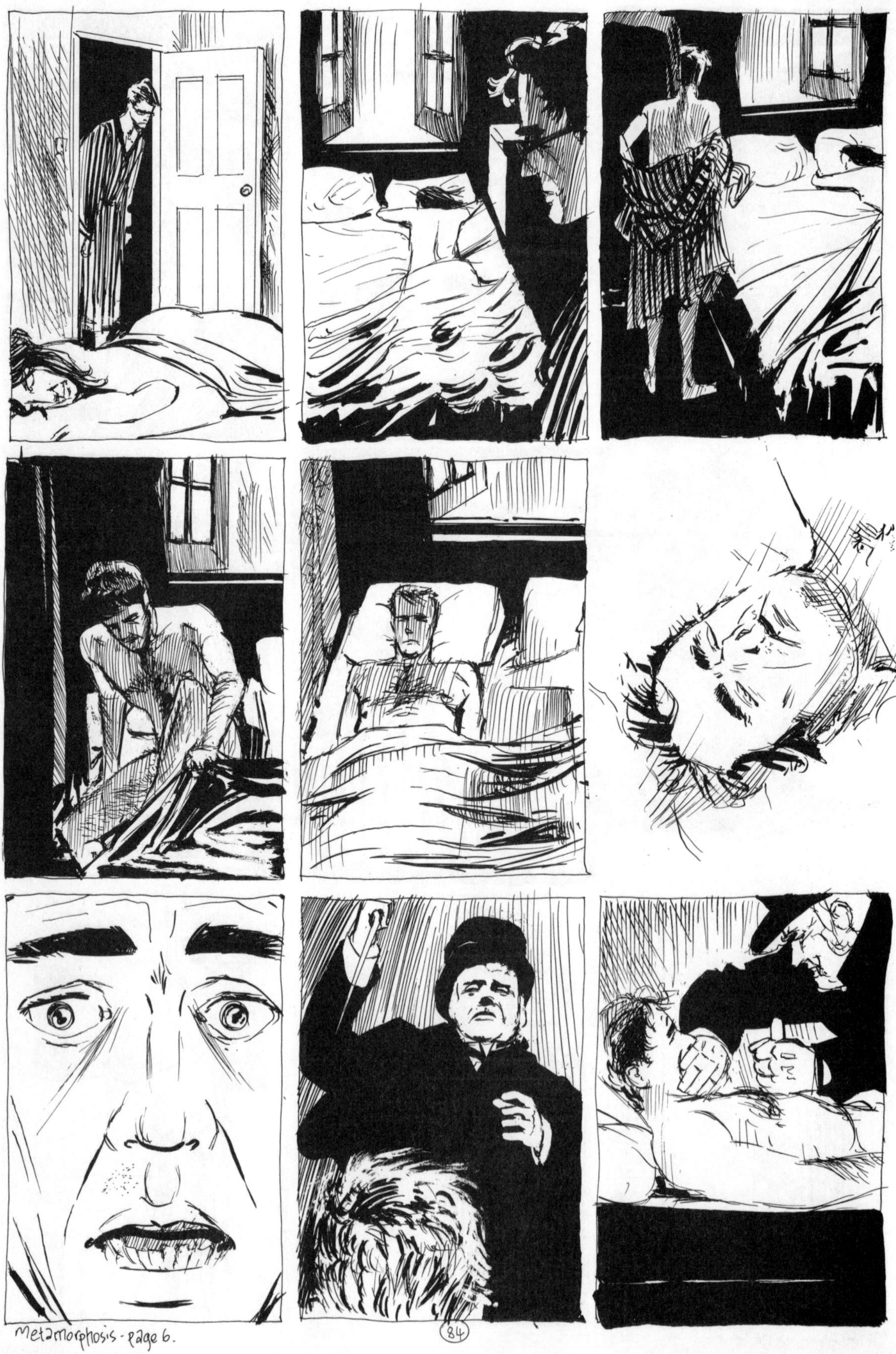

Metamorphosis - page 6.

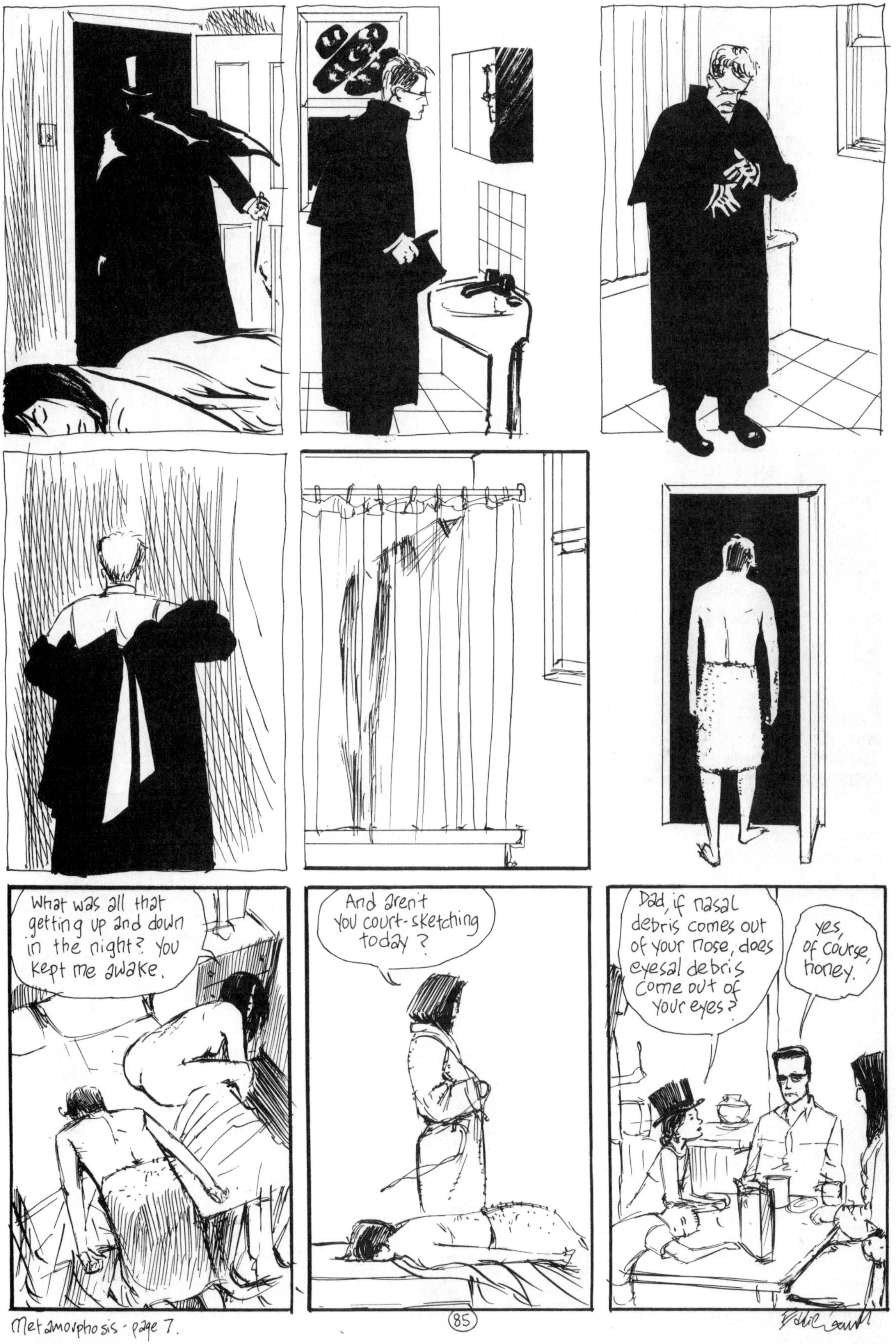
What was all that getting up and down in the night? You kept me awake.
And aren't you court-sketching today?
Dad, if nasal debris comes out of your nose, does eyesal debris come out of your eyes?
yes, of course, honey.

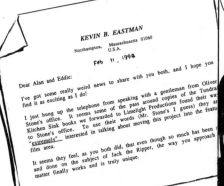

The House that Jack Bought - page 1.

It is an observable effect in the world of movies that whatever stimulus gave rise to the idea of a Jack the Ripper movie in one domain is quite likely to have repeated itself across town.

Thus we hear there is to be a second, concurrent, "Ripper" movie, with Anthony Hopkins in the lead role (fresh from playing Hannibal Lecter) This one's to be based on the recently discovered Diary of the Ripper.

Our movie is dropped due to a lack of interest at the top levels of New Line Cinema and the other one is dropped because the "diary" proves to be a hoax.

Touchstone/Disney take a notion to grab one of these floating Ripper properties, but which to go for? The Comic book or the hoax?

The Comic book comes in just ahead of the hoax, so now the movie's with Touchstone. And then it's with another Mob.

Every time I pull it from the back of my noggin it reels out in a different sequence.

Suddenly it's all a goer and signatures are put on big fat cheques.

"There it is, my honeybee. now you take this cheque and find a big house."

"But look, my love, you take all the time you need. Make comparisons, find one that you like."

The House that Jack Bought - page 2.

I must state here that I've never cared for the idea of owning a house. I just don't get it.

In fact I've always favoured a good and simple rental arrangement.

Is this new concrete driveway to your liking, my good tenant?

Why, it is splendid my fine landlord.

But money paid in rent is wasted money.

How so? Show me the figures.

Look, it just is. Everybody knows that.

Me, I would sooner do business with a fellow human being than with a big faceless banking corporation.

May I plant you some more trees, my good tenant?

No, thanks, but if you would move that one so wifey can get her car out...

So this rigmarole becomes a standing joke over a number of years.

When the dosh arrives, then you must go out and find us...

...a house!

But don't just pick the first one you see, my sweet. The one for us is out there somewhere...

Will you bloody shut up!

The speculation is at an end. The cheque is banked.

The house is sought.

I've found the very house for meee

eh? You only just started looking!

Well, what do you think?

The House that Jack Bought. Page 3.

88

(THE SAME DAY)

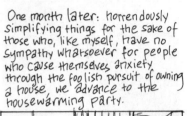

One month later: horrendously simplifying things for the sake of those who, like myself, have no sympathy whatsoever for people who cause themselves anxiety through the foolish pursuit of owning a house, we advance to the housewarming party.

Voodoo.

Eddie Campbell
4.01

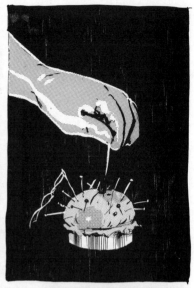

YAWN

What's up?

Aw bloody hell! Kitchen's just gone bust owing us fifteen thousand bucks

The Fan

Eddie Campbell
18. 12. 98.

sigh

When I get to the Irish Club for the show, Paul Furey's leaning on the bar..

So I go through the obligatory muddle:

That can't be him. What's he doing standing out here?

I should say something but maybe he just wants a quiet drink before the show.

Aw, I'm such a fuck-up.

The Fureys are maybe the best pub-band in the world.

After the show he's back at the bar.

Great show! You know, I was standing next to you earlier and didn't know who you were!

Well, I didn't know who you were either.

Ha Ha.

~gloom~
I stood at that bar and nobody knew who I was. my life has been for nothing.

HOT

Campbell

Money

Eddie Campbell.

29.8.98.

Dad, can I have my pocket money?

Yeah. Sure. There you go.

Thanx

Dad... How do you get the money?

Well... let's see. I draw my Stories on these sheets of big paper, see.

Then I send them all to Mr. Printer in Canada in one of these boxes.

And he makes it into lots of comic books like this, thousands all the same, and sends them to Mr. Distributor.

Mr. distributor, now he's in America and he sends the comics to all the shops and every time some Wee person comes in and buys one, some of the money comes back to me.

Yeah, right, Dad HA HA HA

Money - One Page.

Hey, I'm
trying
to get
some
work
done

Eddie Campbell
11 9 98.

the
LaST
Zip-a-**tone**
in
town

Eddie Campbell.
6·00

Big hello to my colleague, Steve Lieber, who sometimes even does convention sketches using the stuff.

I'm buying some zip-a-tones at the art shop. That's those adhesive backed sheets of dot-screen greys; Letratone, Normatone, other brands.

They used to be of some use in the comic strip game.

It's imported and has gotten rather expensive at thirty bucks a sheet way down here. Nowadays everybody 'shades' on the computer.

And you can't find the real McCoy hardly anywhere. It has to be brought in to order.

Hey! Here's a box of leftovers from years ago going for a buck apiece.

And there's not a pattern among

them that I'd use in a

pink fit.

94

The Court Sketcher

Eddie Campbell

Here's the "postcard bandit": a likeable rogue, a Robin Hood.

Massive security operation gree

A prison escapee, he was on the run a long time, supposedly taunting the Police by sending them photo-postcards of himself in famous tourist locations and posing in front of police stations.

He was a master of disguise; he'd do the armed hold-up, run down the street into public toilets where he'd shave off his moustache.

He had a plane seat next to *Jana Wendt*, famous hard-nosed TV journalist and she didn't recognise him with his hair cut short.

MILE-HIGH FLUB: Jana and Brendon Abbott

Scoop came, Wendt

JANA Wendt missed the scoop interview of the year when she didn't recognise Australia's most wanted criminal sitting next to her on a plane.

The ABC spent $1.1 million sending Wendt around the world for interviews for her *Uncensored* series, but her big chance came when armed robber Brendon Abbott joined her in the first-class cabin on a flight to Melbourne.

At the time, a nationwide hunt was on for Abbott, who led the mass break-out from Brisbane's Sir David Longland maximum-security prison last November.

The ABC confirmed the encounter. Wendt did not recognise Abbott, a known master of disguise.

FRANCES WHITING

Now they've nabbed him up north and they're flying him down for processing at the city courthouse.

The streets are crowded. Everybody is out to get a look. But where is the court sketcher?

He was supposed to be on stand-by but he's standing at a bar. He misunderstood the brief. All he can say in his defence is at least he was only drinking a shandy.

And anyway, it's only the postcard bandit. It's not like it's the *kissing bandit* or the *Wet bandits*.

SLIDING DOORS

Eddie Campbell
7/99.

Have you got any dosh? I need a twenty.

What on Earth do you do with it all?!

We've been spending more than we earn for a year and a half - First it's the—

STOP! I don't want to hear it. Go and get your ink!

Haven't you got any cheap, bogus ink?

No sir, and with an Epson printer you should use Epson ink.

Aw, bugger that

Review: Eddie Campbell is a genius. Buy his comic.

Dad, can we eat out tonight

Now, there's a wonderful thought. Let's go to Sizzler.

Look, Real Daddy's caught behind the sliding doors.

Questions

Eddie Campbell
7/4/9

Alright, you lot! You've had a big night and it's school tomorrow. ~hic~... into bed!

Dad, can I take my barbecue beer-bottle tops in for show-and-tell?

hmm...I'll have to think about that one.

Goodnight, honey. I'll see you in your dreams.

Dad...do the King and Queen know each other.

Why, yes, of course, because every night before he goes to sleep he leans over and kisses her and says, "Good night, my fine feathered friend"

Dad, why does he call her that?

Why, because they're the King and Queen of the Cockatoos.

Nighty night.

The Court Sketcher

by

Eddie Campbell

5.14 99.

They found Mr. Sillitoe killed in his cell.

Objection!

We do not know that Mr. Sillitoe was "killed"

What exactly do you mean, Mr. Cuthbert?

There are other ways to die, my Lord, apart from "being killed." One may, for instance, take one's own life.

hmm. Objection sustained

Yes... when Mr. Sillitoe was found dead in his cell, strangled by the electrical cord from the television in a way that I shall demonstr—

My lord, if I may interject at this point. I am concerned about a news "sketch" artist representing my client as being in a cage.

Your client is in a cage, Mr. Johnson.

For his own protection.

Indeed he is, my lord, and I fear that should the public see him thus depicted, it would result in a widespread prejudice against our case.

Does the public not have a right to see things as they are, Mr. Johnson.

Obviously, I have no objection to the...un...."sketching" of my client per se

hmm...and do we have such a "sketcher" in the court today?

Here.

The learned gentleman is clearly familiar with my work, but I would like to reassure him...

...that I drew that thing once and have no intention of tackling it again.

Is that assurance satisfactory to you, Mr. Johnson?

Yes, certainly, my Lord.

Please proceed Mr. Humber.

...strangled by the cord of the television—

Objection!

"Sketched" by "E Campbell"

Dr. Doolittle
by
Eddie Campbell
4.00.

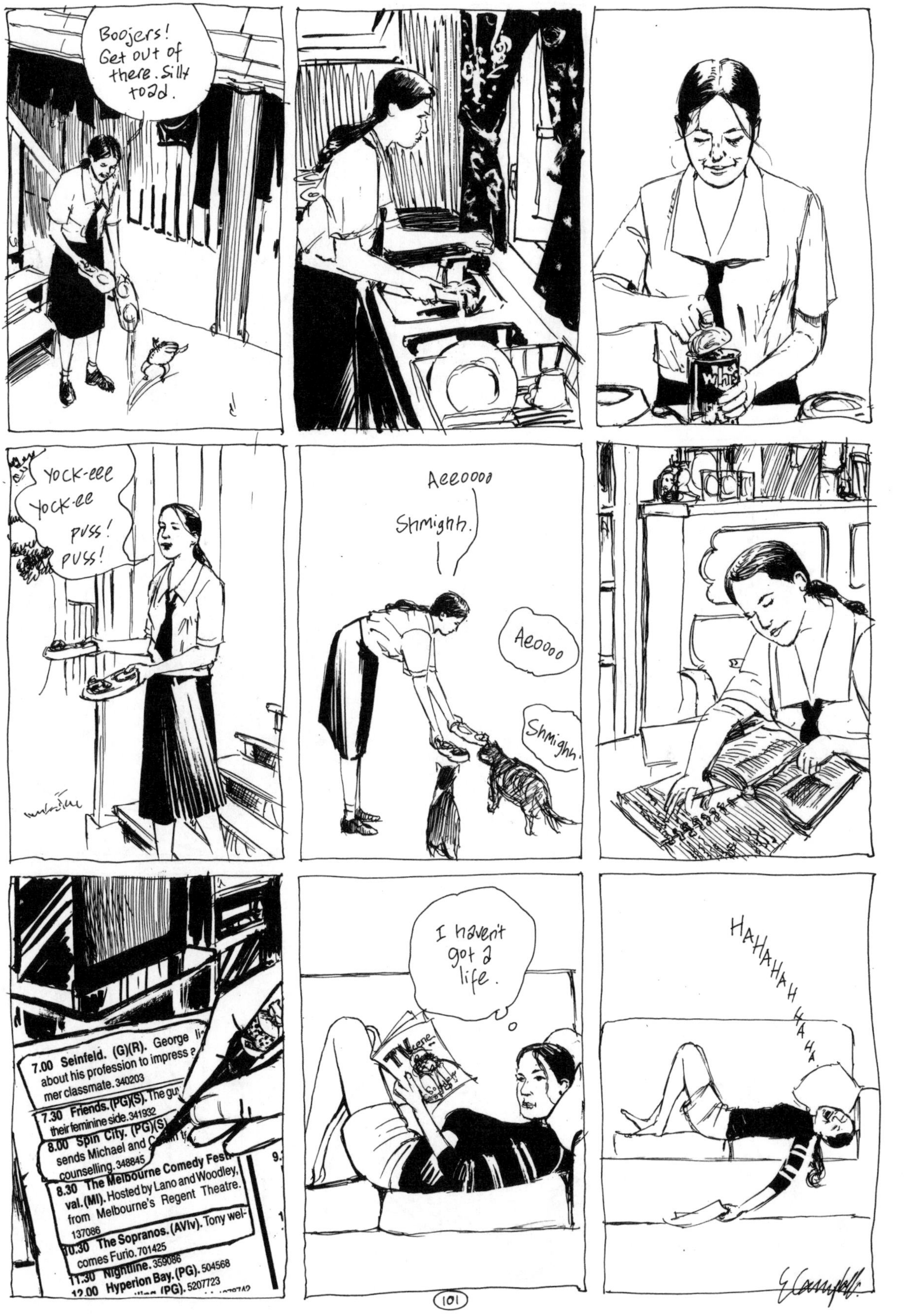
Boojers! Get out of there. Silly toad.
YOCK-eee YOCK-ee puss! puss!
Aeeoooo
Shmighh.
Aeoooo
Shmighh.
7.00 Seinfeld. (G)(R). George li
about his profession to impress a
mer classmate. 340203
7.30 Friends. (PG)(S). The guy
their feminine side. 341932
8.00 Spin City. (PG)(S)
sends Michael and C
counselling. 348845
8.30 The Melbourne Comedy Festi
val. (MI). Hosted by Lano and Woodley,
from Melbourne's Regent Theatre.
137086
10.30 The Sopranos. (AVlv). Tony wel-
comes Furio. 701425
11.30 Nightline. 359086
12.00 Hyperion Bay. (PG). 504568
5207723
I haven't got a life.
HAHAHAHAH HAHA

Eat
your
vegies.

— YES
DAD

Eddie
Campbell
10.00

CALLY! COME
and get your
dinner!

Can't you
do that
later?

It'll just
take a
minute.

CARROTS! Bloody hell!
There's two-week-
old vegetables
under here.

Sit down
and eat
your dinner,
for heaven's
sake.

Aw, geez!
What's this
black gunk?

That's
disgusting

Get back
here this
minute!

smack
him

Bastards.
I have
been...
called.

Eddie Campbell
6/00

"You're such a sullen bastard when you're sober"

"You self-important, patronising bastard."

"YOU'RE A SUPERCILIOUS BASTARD, CAMPBELL"

"Ugh"

"That mischievous bastard over there!"

"That opinionated bastard at the head of the table"

"You thin lipped, disapproving Scot."

"well that was a bit tactless, don't you think!?"

"WAH"

"You lanky streak of piss!"

"WRAUGGHNNBSTARD."

"?"

AND THAT'S JUST THE PEOPLE WHO LIKE ME

Eddie Campbell

Mindsweeping.
Eddie Campbell
10.00

Let me see, I have half an hour. I shall undertake an ontological review of my weltanschauung.

Get a proper helmet you dickhead!

Campbell raids Evans' brain for ideas to pass off as his own.

Have another beer

What do you think of gambling, as a concept?

Isn't it based on the assumption that one can get rich by accident? As a system of belief, I can see no profit in it.

The classification of stuff.

1. Money.

Getting by.

We will help you pay off your mortgage quicker so you can stretch your social status by two and a half inches.

Get knotted

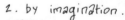

Anomaly: the money going into third world countries as aid is a fraction of that coming out as national debt repayment.

Getting rich.
There are five accredited systems, listed here in descending order
1. by inheritance.

2. by imagination.

WHAT THE CHAMBER MAID SAW.

mindsweeping. page 1

3. by theft.

4. by hard work.

5. by accident.

The Classification of stuff.

2. Body.

Sex gives you AIDS.
Everything else gives you cancer.

Just take me now, Gods.

Around 2005, Lung cancer will overtake breast cancer as the principal killer of women. Smoking diminishes appetite and to women, slimness can be more important than healthiness.

Somewhere else I read that men routinely relinquish responsibility for their own health to their wives.

The diet's not working. We'll try something else.

But don't worry. There's somebody in charge. The Australian Medical Association has made proposals to a federal government enquiry that movies showing smoking should be age-restricted.

Meanwhile, life-expectancy is at its highest since the beginning of human records.

mindsweeping, page 2.

105

The classification of stuff.

3. Nation.

As in so many other places in a modern world where the boundaries of nation disintegrate, a reactionary group arises to reclaim some old imagined dignity.

I am confronted by the proposition, made in all seriousness by one who flies the flag over his front lawn, that, after living here fourteen years, I should by now think of myself as Australian

With all respect, get knotted

The country is awash with national spirit, and also, more anomalies. On the TV news, juxtaposed but no similarity noted, WWII veterans visit sites in Japan and petition for an apology from that government. At home, the Aboriginal community demands an apology from its own government for the 'lost generation' and is rebuffed.

National Front, Neo National Socialist and other "demagogues wrapping themselves in the flag." Here, it's the One Nation Party. The world watches to see if this country is about to embarrass itself.

But no, One Nation fails to get enough votes and in addition is in trouble for electoral fraud.

FIRST THING THE JACK ACID SOCIETY SHOULD DO IS GET RID OF ALL THE BUSYBODIES... ALL THE JOHNNY-COME-LATELIES.

© Kelly-hap.

The great Walt Kelly in the 1950s.

(In my naivete, when I lettered the above caption, I didn't realise she had literally done it. (From photo on their website.)

August 18 1999

One Nation leaders facing fraud charges after

AAP -- Fraud charges may be laid against the One Nation including the ruling trio of Pauline Hanson, David Oldfiel Ettridge, Queensland Premier Peter Beattie said.

Mr Beattie also said the Queensland Electoral Commission action to recover up to $500,000 in public funding the party following last year's state election.

"The Electoral Commission is currently seeking legal advice fro Law as to whether any person should be prosecuted under the Ele for making false and misleading statements," the Premier said.

...ssion will se...

The members start bickering and the organisation splinters after only three years. HA! The *Monster Raving Loony Party* in England has been thriving for three decades

My goodness, even after Sutch popped off?

And when its leader Screaming Lord Sutch died recently, they replaced him with another human and a cat.

JOINT PARTY LEADER

ALAN HOWLING LAUD' HOPE

JOINT PARTY LEADER

CAT-MANDU

PARTY CHAIRMAN

T.C.OWEN

PARTY SECRETARY

MAD COW-GIRL

From their website.

But Australia opens the door to a new era with the High Court's *Mabo* decision of 1992, regarding land rights, which destroyed the legal doctrine of *terra nullius*. It stands as a bright example, attracting from overseas both admiration and delegates to study all the moves for their own benefit.

Eddie Mabo with his lawyers, Murray Island 92.

In the 1940s one Sacheverell Sitwell wrote: "compared to us, the aboriginals are like the muses crowned with flowers... they take part in their ceremonies, we merely sit and gape."

The passage as a whole reeks too much of "the noble savage," but that last bit has lodged itself in my noggin as a biting criticism of modern man.

That reeks a little.

Yes, it does, but... "we merely sit and gape"

The Classification of Stuff

4. Worship.

There are two theories: the Evolution theory and the God Theory

Send twenty five dollars for your free prophecy bible!!

zz

As Hazlitt observed, Netley, "The Gods have gone further off."

On the whole, if you need a god, you could do worse than worship cats.

In 522 bc., the King of Persia, Cambyses II, defeated the Egyptians at Pelusium. Capturing several cats, he used them as shields. The Egyptians, reluctant to wound their sacred cats, surrendered the city.

The magus, he picked a snake.

"If I'm going to adopt a god, I'd rather start out knowing that it was a glove-puppet."

"my imaginary pal"

"It's a fiction. All gods are fiction. It's just that I happen to think fictions are real. Everything around us was once fiction. Before there was the table, there was the idea of the table."

Mindsweeping. page 4.

"If I'm going to be dealing in totally imaginary territory, it struck me that it would be useful to have a native as a guide."

magic:
I had to seek his advice when I took on a short gig writing a magic character. I had no business being in it, of course.

But I concocted the notion of sending Joe Magic off on an occult, binding circle around the world.

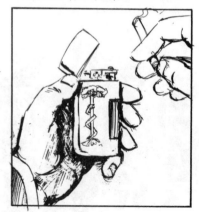

Finally, Nemesis or, just retribution for overconfidence.

The Classification of Stuff.

The 5. Millennium.

That's the state of play as we enter into the new century.

I shall follow Joe Magic in his circle around the planet

I shall tie a bow on the millennium.

Put that in your Weltanschauung and smoke it.

Get Knotted

mindsweeping. page 5.

The Millennium World Tour
of
Eddie Campbell.
9.00.

PART ONE: HE SETS OUT.

The only difficult part of going round the world is in getting out of the house.

It doesn't matter whether I packed this morning or the night before, I still run out the door five minutes later than I should have, get in the car and realise I've forgotten something important.

Hurry up or you'll miss the plane

AAARGH

I'm up for only an hour when the plane has engine trouble and has to come back.

There won't be another flight till tomorrow.

You'll be all right once you're upstairs. You always are.

Let me have my suitcase back then.

I'll see what I can do.

I cheerfully go home.

Aha! I've caught her at it! The sad and awful day has come. Betrayed!

She's filled the kitchen with new furniture and I've only been away two hours.

Yeehah! I live to die another day

You're not supposed to be back!

HEY!!

Hi, Eddie

E Camp

The Millennium World Tour
of
Eddie Campbell
1999!
Singapore.

or

PART TWO: HE SETS OUT AGAIN

A *Singapore Sling* in Raffles Hotel.

It was created there in 1915 by Chinese bartender Ngaim Tong Boon: ½ measure gin, ¼ measure cherry Brandy, ¼ mixed fruit juices (orange, lime, pineapple) a few drops Cointreau and Benedictine, a dash of Angostura Bitters, top with cherry and pineapple.

EIGHTEEN BUCKS! But if you go to Singapore, you have to go to Raffles, and you can't go to Raffles without having a Singapore Sling. It would be bad manners.

Pretend you're with Somerset Maugham and Noel Coward.

I say, who is this insufferable man?

I thought he was your bit of rough

In the hotel where I'm staying, the bar has a six-piece Filipino band. They're good. I don't understand why I'm the only customer.

They're chatting with me. We're having a rare old time.

What shall we play next, Edee?

Beer is nine bucks.

I don't see any drunks.

O inscrutable orient.

E.Campbell.

The Millennium World Tour
of
Eddie Campbell.
1999.

People I don't go
for in a big way.

The guy visiting town who gets me caught up in a conversation and then has to cut out to go look off the bridge or something; just when I'm getting up a head of steam.

oh yes, pointing no fingers

Because he's only here once and has to go and be a tourist and all that.

When he could have been drinking a beer with me. And he's only going to meet me once probably.

Take it for a fact, even. If I see him coming I'll be crossing to the other side.

I went to Australia. Beautiful country. I had a beer with Eddie Campbell.

What did you see there?

Apart from Eddie? hmm.

In the bar of the Excelsior, I get into a conversation with a retired cop who shows me photos of his twelve children. We talk into the wee hours.

you have Tiger, isn't it?

His name is David. He calls me Goliath.

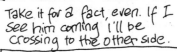

The Millennium World Tour
of
Eddie Campbell.
1999.
M A D R I D.

(nothing works
in Spain)

The baggage carousel
takes an hour to start.

When it starts, the first thing
out is a shampoo bottle

David Macho's been waiting ages
to pick me up. The police have
taken his car away.

*#!/#

Big Jim Hudnall's bags don't come
off the carousel at all. Lesson:
always wear your best clothes
on the plane.

Dave Gibbons is here, amused to
still be signing copies of the
eleven year old WATCHMEN as
though it's just out. With Jaime
Delano we go through the PRADO
composing dialogue for the
characters in the paintings.

(and the modern museum too)

Hugo, our official translator,
works overtime.

tell her she
has pretty eyes

Edee,
I wish
to sleep

On the second evening in the
hotel I find that all the soap's
been removed from my room.

Where's my
soap gone?

Que?

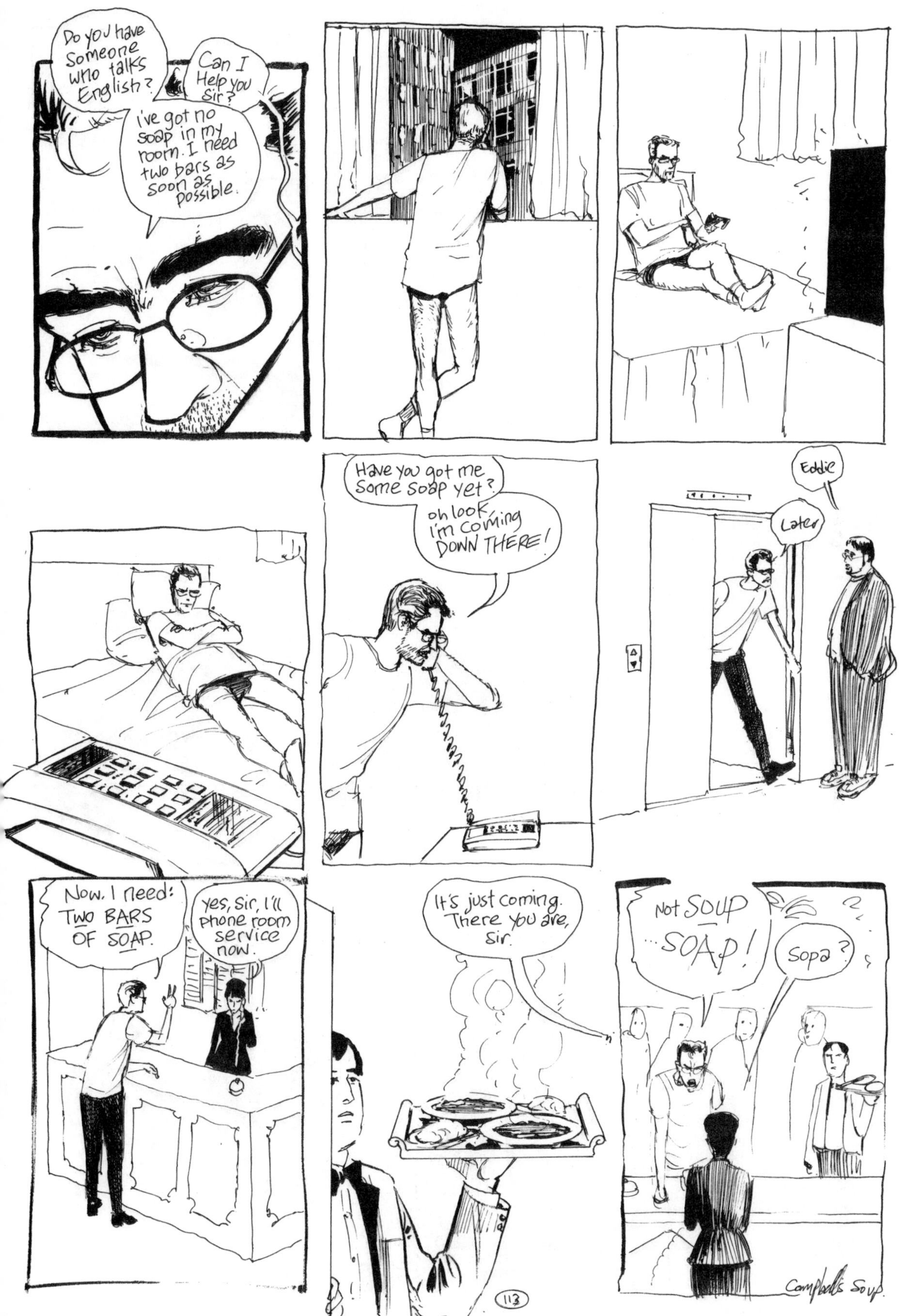

Do you have Someone who talks English?
Can I Help you Sir?
i've got no soap in my room. I need two bars as soon as possible.
Have you got me some soap yet?
oh look I'm coming DOWN THERE!
Eddie
Later
Now. I need: TWO BARS OF SOAP.
yes, sir, I'll phone room service now.
It's just coming. There you are, sir.
Not SOUP ...SOAP!
Sopa?
Campbell's Soup

The Millennium World Tour of *Eddie Campbell*, one of several foreign guests in Madrid.

1999

David Macho's telling me:

You'll be at the awards ceremony, of course you will. It's at a disco.

Discos are not my scene.

You'll love it. We've got a stripper and transvestites on stilts.

transvestites on stilts.

It's in Tres Cantos, a concrete New Town satellite of Madrid.

Everywhere I go on the planet, Kurt Busiek's there ahead of me getting an award. He's wearing spanking new white trainers that look like big baby-bootees under the disco lights.

Then they give some plaques and certificates to people I've never heard of while I'm getting a round of gins and tonics. And finally, there's the lifetime achievement award for an old cartoonist in his eighties.

He's a local hero who fought by Castro's side in Cuba. A hum of awe goes round the place: standing ovation.

He's shakily getting off the stage when the transvestites arrive.

And the smoke bombs go off.

114

Eddie Campbell.

The Millennium World Tour
of
Eddie Campbell.
1999
in transit.

London Heathrow, British Midland lounge. The screen directs flyers to the right gates. It's telling me to "Wait in this lounge". I imagine it will say "now boarding" when the time comes, but this does not happen and I fail to hear the loudspeakers call my flight.

Even when they call a bunch of names including Campbell, I think "gee, those guys are so cool they get a personal wake-up call. Only when I hear "Eddie Campbell" does the coincidence seem stretched.

I was sitting over there waiting for three hours! honest.

I think you just called me. Eddie Campbell?

huh?

Mister, I've been calling you for ten minutes! Where have you been?

Just over there!

Okay. When's the next one?

two hours

hmm... my bag's on this one. Can I make sure somebody holds it for me in Manchester?

You're bag's on this one?..Oh... hold on

We really shouldn't be doing this!

HURRY

SAFETY

The captain wants to speak to you

Congratulations. for keeping us all late.

This is not funny, you know.

home again
home again
jiggery jig

I visit my parents for two weeks. This Millennium World Tour thingy is no more than an excuse to revisit the various phases of my life.

Me keeping the plane late has already caused trouble in mum's neatly arranged life. It takes a few days to smooth things out.

Meals are at nine, one and five. To carve out enough time to get something done, you'd have to cancel one of the meals.

In my noodle, I contrast Spain, with its siesta and its cheery disregard for the sober concept of time, and in Spain you get even less done.

I don't leave the house except to go to the post office and the off-licence, for wine.

I turn up for all meals. A third week of this and I'd find myself inadvertently asking for a raise in my pocket money.

In the evenings I watch TV with my parents and see for myself why the oldies develop such a pessimistic view of the world

Finally, when I leave

The Millenium World Tour
of
Eddie Campbell.
1999.

An Evening
with the
Magus.

haze.

Stratus

cumulus

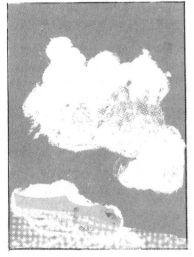

Cumulonimbus

Stormy billows

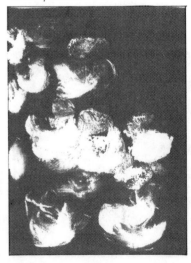

Waves

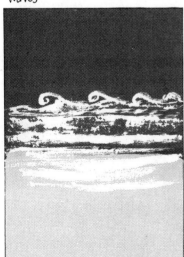

Cirrus

Halo and parhelia

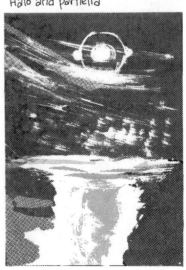

Auld lang syne

by

Eddie Campbell

9-99.

In my narratives I used to call him Danny Grey because I had a notion the statute of limitations was still open on a couple of his past misdemeanors. He'd already changed his name once himself.

And misdemeanors were being added. Like the time he clocked an annoying guy in the car park of the *Dickens*, knocking him out cold and then we had to tear away at high speed.

I scoured the local papers next morning, hoping to find no reference to the silly bastard coming to serious grief lying there in the dark.

At 49 Bob's looking older than I want him to. The white wine is chilled and on the table. The red is breathing on the mantelpiece where I should expect to find it.

He and his wife have divorced since I last caught up with him five years ago when I sent a message to meet at the *Cat and Fiddle*, a pub high in Derbyshire which neither of us had ever visited. The arrangement had an obliqueness that would have excited him in the old days.

He gets around plenty. Has a sweetie in Russia; took another one to Cuba. Took time out from driving elevated platform trucks to be a vet's assistant for a year.

I give him a couple of my latest books. He runs his severely critical eye over them and having gotten that apparently necessary ritual out of the way, we get down to the regular business.

In the morning we resume our places and remain there all day.

Wee Eddie would have lapped it up, imagining a day when the world might give him leave to be in stories instead of reading them in comics or watching them on the TV

The stories all connect with a river-side pub situated in the uncomplicated magic night. I called it the *King Canute* when my narrative technique was less certain.

Everybody met everybody else at this *King Canute*. Bob met his wife there; I met Penny Moore. She met somebody else. By this time it had gotten complicated

Penny Moore married our old pal, George Waite. I'm looking at the photographs.

They look happy. It lasted all of five months.

Next day we visit the old pub. It seems very sedate now.

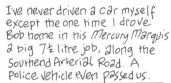

In the car park I recall a car I bought for Penny: a *Hilman Husky*, for $3500, which was less than half my week's wages. I had to get Bob to drive it to here for me. It sat outside the pub for months till we got complaints.

Apparently there was a problem with the cooling system. I got John Godfrey to look at it for me. He poured in two pints of water and watched it all come out of the exhaust pipe.

I've never driven a car myself except the one time I drove Bob home in his *Mercury Marquis* a big 7½ litre job, along the Southend Arterial Road. A Police vehicle even passed us.

So we take the van and drive somewhere to try for a live-in job with her looking after the horses and me as a handyman. Of all the fictions I've written, this I believed in the least.

To divorce oneself from the fiction without going straight into another is the trick; to avoid getting stuck in a genre.

In another album I find photos of our dark-haired youth which I haven't seen before. It's like finding one of those issues I once searched for in vain all over town.

Perhaps there are plot twists in here that still might surprise me;

Rare outtakes. variant endings. So much of it that I imagine the story might still be running somewhere

Just for my benefit.

(Bob's wife, Sue).

The photograph is the greatest fiction of all. What would the ancient image makers think of it, as they strove to compose their symbolism to perfectly represent the eternal and immutable?

My hero of twenty five years ago looks at me over the top of his reading glasses. How I've missed him.

NOW, LOOK HERE SMARTARSE. BRITANNICA SAYS...

Eddie Campbell

The Dog Whisperer

Eddie Campbell

5 - 00

All the way to the airport I'm picturing Bob sending doggies resignedly off to oblivion.

CHUCKETYBRUM CHUCKETYBRUM

Whispering to them things that Bob and dogs know while the vet injects the lethal dose.

He gave up his job training people to operate elevated platform trucks in one of those moments...

...that grab us...

...in this phase of life.

Then while taking one of his own dogs to the vet he cheerfully offered himself as a cheap assistant.

chucketybrum, chucketybrum. We're watching television one night twenty or so years ago.

I don't care how honest it is; it's too horrible to think of

Penelope Keith's one of the sexiest women alive.

(Noel Coward's Private Lives)

Let's be superficial and pity the poor philosophers. Let's blow trumpets and squeakers and enjoy the party like small quite idiotic school children. Come and kiss me, darling before your body rots and worms pop in and out of your eye sockets

Worms don't pop.

Isn't this so redolent of sex. But if it was a modern play, by now you'd see them on the setee with his spotty arse bobbing up and down

chuckety brum, chuckety brum. It's a long old ride out to Heathrow, but being permitted to sit and do nothing is such a luxury these days.

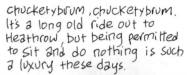

For three or four years Bob and I used to just mooch around wherever the whim took us. I made a book about it.

I recall one night we took Beryl from the factory out to dinner in appreciation of all the apple pies she used to bake for us.

oh good lord NO!

The Dog Whisperer. page 2.

122

Chucketybrum, chucketybrum.
There's always been some kind
of story trying to happen around
Bob. I wistfully think about
all the ones I've missed.

chucketybrum, chucketybrum.

The Dog Whisperer · page 4

The Millennium World Tour of Eddie Campbell.

p a r t   n i n e t e e n

The Organizer

Next stop is Georgia, U.S.A. My buddy Chris Staros is waiting. He already knows which carousel the bags will be on and how to get to it. He's my organizer.

He's also the perfect example of how Fate will send you the one you need right when the need is upon you.

Just after I announced I was going to be my own publisher, he popped up in the mail offering to represent me in the States.

It was two years before we met in the flesh, to do a convention. I upset his sense of order when I invited a didgeridoo player into our booth.

I turn my back for one minute...

By this time he was so adept at promoting my books that he didn't need me in among it. Nevertheless, we're pulling in a bundle. I'm sticking it all in the little safe in the hotel room.

I'm already doing statistics: divide this day's from yesterday's with a baggage tag, this thousand from that with a boarding pass. Separate the float with a lunch receipt.

Next day same routine, and stick in a memo for cash taken out for down payment on an ad. Do a quick calculation. Yes, very good indeed. Graphs and charts are already forming in my noodle: best time to man the booth, to be away, etc.

dUm de doo de da.

Chris has to go in for some change.

Aw, poor Eddie; he's only an artist. I'll fix it for him.

Oh well...

So now he's a partner in running a publishing operation called Topshelf. For his day job he's a manager at Lockheed. He used to be a heavy metal guitarist (I've seen the video)

Staros gets me on my plane to N.Y.

It's strange revisiting smallpressdom this late in the day. The daft enthusiasm of it all. O me, where is the life I led.?

(I'm leaving in the twin towers)

Nita Staros has every corner of the house looking like a photo from Better Homes and Gardens.

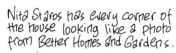

Then by a mysterious sleight of hand he's waiting for me when I get there.

Way back in '76 I was in N.Y. with my first wee silly hand-made comic, too afraid to go in anywhere.

Oh, what luxury. There are a zillion e-mails from my kids and other stuff. A magazine wants a phone interview. Time is arranged. Shop appearance in New York. Contents of a speech in Maryland to be discussed...

The schedule is all pinned down. In N.Y. I'm meeting all these small press guys. Sleeping bag days are here again.

But how pleasing it is to go visiting when you're not selling anything. So we drop in on Superman, and Vertigo, and all that...

The Organizer · page 2.

The big 600 page From Hell will be out for Christmas. I'm sure the lovely Karen Berger thinks Chris is the publisher. Nobody wants to believe that the illustrator can publish too.

But then, maybe it's because I got off the last plane deaf in one ear. I just came down Third Avenue like walking under water

Maybe I'm missing some of the conversation and Chris is holding up my end for me. Who knows what's going on out there?

It's like being sozzled. And the lovely Karen Berger could be the queen of the bottom of the sea. We're showing pictures of our children.

All life has lately become a big daft stage. Nothing's real.

Next day we almost truly are walking under water. Hurricane Floyd is pissing up and down the coast.

We're stuck on an immobile train halfway to Washington D.C. Temporary suspension of the normal schedule can bring out the best in people.

Then we're all ushered off the train and onto a bus. Why, oh why did I pick up all those damn books at my parents' house? Forty four and still going home for my things.

Bethesda, Maryland. Staros is sorting out the room bookings. He's got it so that the home team are paying for mine, except some wires have got crossed.

This first room should already be taken care of.

The Organizer. page 3

He's got it all ship-shape in no time.

"ICAF will take care of the room as you're doing the speech. Greg and Joel have defrayed your travel expense to get you to SPX. So you give them a box of books..."

"Good idea"

ICAF: International Cartoon Arts Festival.
SPX: Small Press Expo.

He's the emcee at the Ignatz awards:

"Our next presenter has been creating graphic novels for a quarter of a century!"

"You don't look that old."

"MY GOODNESS, IGNATZ"

"Nix with the quarter century."

"YOU ARE DEVELOPING A KALF UPON ONE OF YOUR LIMBS"

"It's an actual brick!"

"Now I realize why you never sent the one I won two years ago."

"We've still got it at the shop— I'll get it to you tomorrow"

"ZING"

"THATS WHERE A BEE BIT ME, SILLY"

While I'm relaxing in the glow of the moment, one Victor Cayro plonks himself next to me. I ran one of his drawings in a recent issue of my magazine.

"You bitches don't even fuckin' know who this is! He taught us everything."

"He forgot to teach you some manners"

Cayro is gulping his way through all the stages of intoxication in one six-pack which he has smuggled into the function.

"Now what were they again... verbose, jocose, bellicose, morose, lachrymose."

Next time I see him he's asleep in an armchair in the lobby.

"Comatose!"

"Z"

There's a genuine jolly old party upstairs with a jacuzzi—full of beer and cider.

Some wags have carried Cayro in his armchair into one of the elevators where he goes up and down all night.

Staros has got three rooms including this one and he's juggling all his artists in and out in different permutations.

Then in the morning he's away early.

I'm trying to remember why I booked my flight out so late in the day. Oh yes! The last time I woke up with a sore head and Chris had to reorganize my flights

I have brunch with Connie, that delightful lady who happens to also be Quentin Tarantino's mom, and Neil. I've managed to catch up with just about everyone on this tour.

Then they're all off in a limo to watch Neil introduce the special preview showing of *Princess Mononoke*.

To Hell with it, I'll wait at the airport.

Nothing's real. Take a bow.

Eternity

Eddie Campbell
3/2000

It's a friendly, safe feeling, arriving home to a warm, humid place. Is it just familiarity, or a womb-thing? Or the memory of the anticipation of a hot-climate holiday.

First order of the day is to get the huge *From Hell* off to the printer.

There's another sleepless night while the finished books go out of Canada filling up an eighteen-wheeler.

With a wholesale value higher than the cost of our house, it runs off the road.

It is hijacked and blown up on the order of the Freemasons.

It'll murder me.

I've decided to drink sensibly this party season.

Eternity - page 1

The usual big Dickensian Christmas dinner has a way of keeping the booze in its place.

We attempt the same strategy on New Year's Eve, taking the whole party to a restaurant that closes at eleven.

Then we drive up the mountain to watch the fireworks over the city. Mullins tells me the pyrotechnicians have reset their computers to 1998 to outwit the 'millennium bug'.

Now the countdown. There it goes. End of a millennium.

"...we'll take a cup o' kindness yet, for the sake of Auld Lang Syne."

"uh how does the rest go? we're here because we're here because..."

Aw no, we've forgotten the words !!!? How did that happen? Annie and I usually photocopy the sheet music and hand it out.

We twa hae run aboot the braes And pulled the gowans fine

...fields and plucked the daisies...

It's almost tragic. It's one of the three most popular songs in the English speaking world along with Happy Birthday and For He's a Jolly Good Fellow (as we call it in our house).

We've wandered mony a weary foot Since Auld Lang Syne

Words by BURNS.

Not too slow.

Voice.

Piano. mf

Robert Burns, dying at the age of 37 in 1796; could he have imagined the celebrity of his verses?

We twa hae paidl'd in the burn, From morning sun till dine

...paddled in the stream

Carried in Romantic feeling to the corners of the English speaking world.

But seas between us braid hae roared Since Auld Lang Syne.

...broad have roared

I feel like I've left a country I was quite fond of, the twentieth century, heading over Burns' broad roaring seas.

A stretch limo passes. There's a big trade in limo hire tonight. Surely the point is to be in the picture, not gaping at it through dark glass.

All the way down the mountain I'm thinking something's missing. Observances have not been made.

The night is descending into bathos. Mick has to urinate in the vicinity of the graveyard.

DON'T LET MICK BACK IN THE CAR! HE'S A ZOMBIE NOW!

QUICK MUM! DRIVE!

Evans is one of those who are still insisting it's not even the one true millennium.

Do your sums! It's next year.

The date is arbitrary! Anyone who'd save year that they could have now is no devotee of Bacchus!

Bacchus?! But you're just a disapproving, thin-lipped Scot!

I had a notion the millennium night would be so good that it would entertain me instead of the other way around. Feeling I have let it down, I sit up into the wee hours watching the global television coverage. The sun is setting on Easter Island.

In New Orleans they're giving the old millennium a funeral

Eternity - page 3.

They re-show the Sydney bridge fireworks. A word burns itself on my retina, and perhaps on the retinae of two billion others.

And therein lies a story: it was a message that Arthur Stace, reformed criminal and recovered alcoholic, chalked almost everywhere in Sydney between his rebirth into Christianity in 1930 and his death in 1967

Given his medium, most of his work washed off within a few days, but one example remains inside the big bell at Sydney's Martin Place, where it appeared in 1963.

Sydney poet Douglas Stewart wrote: "That shy, mysterious poet, Arthur Stace, whose work was just one single, mighty word, Worked in the utmost depths of time and space...

The fireworks go off around the planet in the same order that I did: Singapore, Madrid, New York. There's a baptism at sunrise by the Jordan in a combined Catholic-Jordanian ceremony.

In Africa, Nelson Mandela lights a candle in the cell where he was incarcerated for twenty-five years, and passes it to the young generation

In the Amazon jungle they dance to their anaconda god. It looks like a perfectly natural conga line.

It's too late for me to believe in anything enough to dance with such fervent abandon. And it's too late tonight to do anything symbolically significant.

But I'll be damned if I'm going to bed yet.

Ma, let's take ourselves under the trees by the creek and make love as the sun comes up.

Okay, Pa. Let's paddle in the burrn.

So we go over to the woods, which is a bird sanctuary, or so they told us when they sold us the house, and we take off all our clothes...

In full sight of the kookaburra, the sulphur crested cockatoo, the tawny frogmouth owl, the galah, the lorikeet, a bird which in our house we call the boojer bird and a bird who sings the first two bars of the can-can.

Eddie Campbell

Eternity-page 4

Mick's Grave New World

Eddie Campbell
11.00

Two thousand A.D.! In the seventies we imagined it would be a future of bubble-shaped anti-gravity cars.

With sky-ways linking the tops of strange expressionist buildings that even Mies van der Rohe couldn't conceive.

We thought we'd be dressing in tin-foil clothes but instead i'm looking at fucking brown corduroy with elbow patches.

Here we are in two fucking thousand with more cunts walking about than in the nineteen seventies.

We were supposed to have replicants of ourselves to perform all our works while we bask in the glory.

Instead we've got third world countries turning out ugly sports training shoes.

No glittering spires; no end to global warming; no unified world economy; no cures for AIDS or cancer. no cryogenic immortality!

But. it's the silvery suits I miss the most.

Campbell

Parents: Pity the poor fools.

Eddie Campbell 3.01

Fathers complain about being out at work and missing all those salient moments in their children's upbringing. Well, this is true for me too and I work at home.

There's a half hour at the end of the day when I run up to the post office. We've arranged it this way so that I get some daily exercise.

But it's during this half hour zone that all the calamities in our house have happened. All three of our children have been hospitalized and all three during this half hour of the day.

I arrive home from the Post Office to find glass all over the verandah and half-eaten sandwiches on the table. It's like they've all been beamed up by aliens.

I panic and start phoning the doctor and hospital.

Only a half hour before, my son Callum locked my daughter Hayley out of the front door and, as if that weren't enough, made faces at her from the window.

LET ME IN!

HA HA FUCK YOU!

She got so mad she punched the glass out of the door and ripped her wrist open.

I'M GONNA KILL YOU!

AAAAAAAA

The shout was heard a mile away.

Whither yon blood-curdling scream?

Parents. Pity Them.

Eddie

I've got mail!

"Pay off your mortgage in five years.

Lose 15 pounds in a week...

Do you like hot sex?

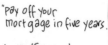

Eddie Campbell
4.01

Hey, Erin! Look at this. It's vagina.com

Oh my God! that's disgusting

Hee Hee . Tt. Ooon . Holee... Oh my God T+. WAH! HeeHee He Oooo . Where's she putting that? Oh my god...

What's going on here? What's all the noise?

AAA! We're sprung!

It was him it wasn't me!

RUN!

Eddie. This is serious. Look what they've been up to.

Amazing! How did they figure that out? You can take any word and put 'dotcom' after it.

That's awful. Can you go and have a talk to them?

Yes. We can't have this going on.

Tut tut.

hmm...

penis.com.

Eddie

Cider in Asturias.

by Eddie Campbell 8/00

Here I am in Spain again. A suitcase falls off the baggage truck.

How will they deal with it, I wonder. Ah yes, here comes a jeep chasing the truck.

The truck driver can't hear a thing, so the jeep fetches the case.

And rides back, balancing it on the bonnet.

From Madrid to Asturias in Northern Spain. Here, cider (sidre) is the traditional drink. It's a particularly flat and cloudy variant of cider.

It is drunk, of course, in the Sidrerias.

Very friendly little places indeed. Notice nobody is holding a glass. The same one gets passed around a group, with a new mouthful in the bottom of it, poured for each person. Any cider remaining in the glass after your mouthful should be tossed into the trough at the foot of the bar.

The cider must be poured from high up, or, more specifically, thrown. Presumably, this is to aerate and enliven it. No other method is acceptable.

It is to be chucked back immediately after pouring, as explained to me by my translator and drinking buddy for the week, Nino Ortea.

> How do I order a refill?

> Eddie, you ask for a "Culin", which means a um... "small bottom" but be careful...

I've been asked to do a front cover for the festival's journal. So I tape paper to the bathroom wall and paint myself practicing the throwing technique the way Nino says he learned as a kid.

We deliver the picture and go for more cider. It's all eat, drink and smoke here. And the rain in Spain falls mainly in this street.

At the pomologica, or cider research centre, out in the country, there are computers and test tubes everywhere, but I'm intrigued by a device on the wall of the recreation room for mechanically throwing the cider.

My host Norman Fernandez

The week ends with a Sunday picnic where more cider is to be chucked. I'm up to my ankles in cider.

I dress knowing these things always end in a ball game.

and in Spain, the ritual embarrassing of the guests.

> I thought I was just going to have to throw the cider

Then everybody sings an old sentimental song...

> Adios con el corazon
> que con el alma no puedo.

as the coach takes away those guests bound by road for Madrid.

> Al despedirme de ti
> Al despedirme me muero.

Cider in Asturias – page 2. "Farewell with all my heart, because I can't say it with my soul. When I say goodbye to you, when I say goodbye to you, I feel like dying." or so Nino says, on the back of a handy coaster

THE TOPSHELF BOYS

We also have stickers, coasters, matchboxes and posters to help enhance Topshelf's presence in your store.

Eddie Campbell 8.00.

I have to catch the next plane out. I don't think Nita's dad will see out the day.

Aw, we're all on a bus to shitsville, man.

Chris

Brett

So you're going to have to sell this to the retailers.

Hey, no sweat.

Now the package contains only our BEST SELLING GRAPHIC NOVELS, with a total retail value of FIVE...HUNDRED...DOLLARS. THEY only have to pay TWO-TWO-FIVE

Cool.

That's 55% off!! FIFTY FIVE PER CENT!

Discount City, man.

We're even going to ship the books at our OWN expense

Awesome

They don't even have to pay for THIRTY DAYS! We'll invoice them.

Wow

And not only that, but any books they can't sell after ninety days we'll replace with anything else from the catalog of an equivalent value!

Have you got all that? Play it back to me.

Okay

Hey, dude! Here's the spiel on the deal...

139

In Wallyhood I audition for all kinds of roles.

In WALLYHOOD

Eddie Campbell 8/00.

Different lives.

Different deaths.

"LOOK, ma! Top of da WOILD! KA BOOM"

I'm eyeing off the leading ladies.

Check all the gear back into the costume dept. and start over

In this one, an exhibitionist.

In the next one, an inhibitionist.

Did I look stupid?

It was funny at first

The script gets numerous rewrites.

I watch it all in the rushes.

oh no. oh no.

Oh Bloody blatherin' Poo.

More lives

More deaths.

"Not waving but drowning"

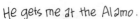

(Death too reads for parts in Wallyhood.)

I grapple with my nemesis. over Reichenbach Falls

He gets me at the Alamo.

Then one day we all may wake up and find that we're stereotyped.

In Wallyhood the plot starts with a good idea and ends with a cliché.

In Wallyhood· page 2.

Which cliché? How about the revenge scenario, in which, say, a great set-piece, a shoot-out on the stairs at Chicago's rail station, is superceded by a dumb finale on a rooftop.

The sadistic bastard goes off it. That's when I'm in *The Untouchables*. Where do they get this crap? Out of comic books? Don't laugh.

Another movie I can't watch to the end is *The Patriot*. It became a moot point with me, whether it buggered around too much with history...

When I absentmindedly wandered out of the cinema fifteen minutes from the end, having lost all interest in the futures of the characters.

It might as well have been *Aliens*, another movie I have to turn off early.

What is it with the revenge scenario? Why does the viewer desire to be manipulated in this way? Who are they getting vicarious revenge upon; themselves?

You idiots! Get outta here.

Have I become very moral? Indeed the greatest play in the English language was a 'revenge tragedy'. In taking his revenge, Hamlet must by all the rules be killed himself and probably go to Hell.

Die ya bastard. Garhhh. YAH!

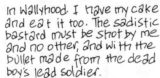

In Wallyhood I have my cake and eat it too. The sadistic bastard must be shot by me and no other, and with the bullet made from the dead boy's lead soldier.

And then I go and marry Aunt Charlotte. At least, that's how it must end under the modern rules of play. And the rules are fixed. Nothing random here, thank God. It's all conspiracy theories and Wallyhood gossip and second endings.

The meter says more dumbness. Crank it up!

dumbmeter editomatic.

In Wallyhood · page 3

Then all the poor dead people who were in the church when the sadistic bastard ordered the doors locked and the torch set upon it, they come out of their trailers for the wrap party.

The Snooter has to leave early for a location shoot in Prague

The triumph of Eddie Campbell.

AW FUCK
AW no.
AW geez..
NN GH
GOD. AW
cum

I read the previews.

Leo
July 24–August 23
These past seven days and those to come represent a period when what was once unchanging and unchangeable is utterly transformed—especially for those with a birthday on or near August 11. Tuesday's full moon falls in the relationship sector, so a partner requires extra understanding. But this also has the capacity reveal to

Scorpio
October 24–Novem
Are you enjoyi
roller-coaster rid
aspects range fro
great to the gha
could be soar
meting. N
same ma
it is non
if your
Nover
chan

In Wallyhood - page 4

143

Monty the dog.

Eddie Campbell 3.01

When we moved into this house we found some attractive fixtures left for us, including the beautiful cream coloured curtains that make our bedroom look very bridal.

A dishwasher I hardly ever use because doing it by hand takes half the effort

And on the gate, a good example of one of the more inventive BEWARE OF THE DOG signs.

I left it there for its attractiveness.

Later I found that it served the same purpose as a real dog.

I can make the gate in six seconds. How fast are you?

In conds fast you?

Hallo!! Are you coming down?

That doesn't wash with the kids

A year before the infernal day.

Six months before the woeful decision.

But you said that one day...

Yeah sure. one day.

You can't keep putting off the decision.

We can put it off as long as we like.

You've no intention of buying a dog, have you!

You're just playing with our feelings.

Monty the Dog - page 1

One hour before the irreversible action.
Hey, Why don't we get a dog?
This is a wind-up, isn't it?
Do you mean it?
The brief window of opportunity during which my life might still go the way I planned it.
you've gone quiet.
Aw, you poor wee guy; you're lonely.
OWCH!
you bloody dog
Go
To
sleep
AAAA

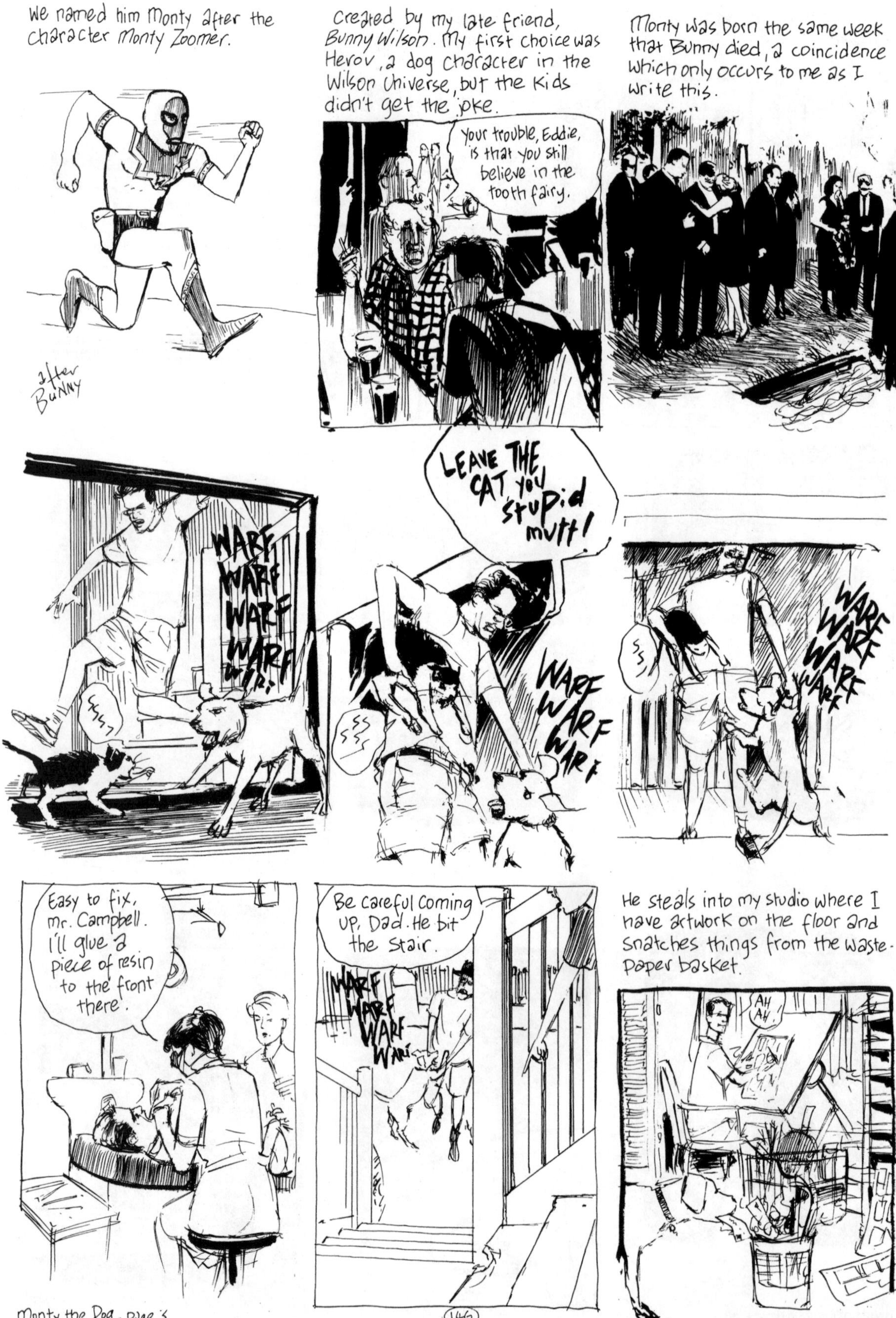

We named him Monty after the character Monty Zoomer.
after BUNNY
Created by my late friend, Bunny Wilson. My first choice was Herov, a dog character in the Wilson Universe, but the kids didn't get the joke.
Your trouble, Eddie, is that you still believe in the tooth fairy.
Monty was born the same week that Bunny died, a coincidence which only occurs to me as I write this.
WARF WARF WARF WARF WARF
LEAVE THE CAT YOU STUPID MUTT!
WARF WARF WARF
WARF WARF WARF WARF
Easy to fix, Mr. Campbell. I'll glue a piece of resin to the front there.
Be careful coming up, Dad. He bit the stair.
WARF WARF WARF WARF
He steals into my studio where I have artwork on the floor and snatches things from the waste-paper basket.
AH AH!

In his dog brain he thinks the papers in the bright container must be important to me. I do not discourage this line of thought.

PUT IT BACK!

In the park.

NO!

STOP HIM, MUM! He's dakking the jogger

You see, psychologically, he's now a member of our pack and he's jostling for position.

your dog

It is my son's ambition to get to a higher position than the dog in the pack structure.

oi!

And so life settles into a new pattern.

I think of Bunny in the grave, with nothing going on.

And I arrive home to screaming chaos.

Dad! When are you getting Monty desexed?

I get up one Sunday Morning to find my gate vandalized and the dog sign gone.

I the SI Ha are

For two years we had a dog sign but no dog. Two months after buying a dog, the sign disappears. Never question these things.

MAIL

THiS Enlightened Consumer Age

We bought a border collie, but it was out of control in our small yard.

So we took it to the pound.

Took it to the pound.

Took it to the pound.

The convenience of the consumer society. Everything can be returned to the store.

The customer's always right.

AAAAA! WHO LET THE DOG IN!?

WAKE WARF

Trade in your old vacuum cleaner, car... your small breasts for big ones. your face for somebody else's.

Trade in your marriage for a divorce.

your pregnancy for an abortion.

AAAAAAAA

Take your neurosis to the shrink. Your obesity to the dietician.

Your mother to the retirement home.

Is the weather to your satisfaction?

more rain?

It's shocking.

God's doing shoddy work in Borneo

I've a good mind to take my custom elsewhere

A PARABLE

Meanwhile, in a village long ago, on a certain evening every year, each of the villagers wraps his or her cares in a bundle and amid much ceremony they place them all around the village fountain.

Then they retire to their abodes free of all that worried them and corroded their peace of mind.

On the next day, the burgomeister's officials will, as per the old custom, redistribute the bundles arbitrarily among the cottages, promoting cohesion in the community, and a refreshment of spirit.

However, on that morning each year, just before dawn, all of the villagers steal out early to the fountain...

..to make certain of getting back their own bundle.

Eddie

Old Man's Town.

The fields of youth are filled with flowers
   The wine of youth is strong.
What need have we to count the hours,
   The summer days are long.

But soon we find to our dismay
   That we are drifting down
The barren slopes that fall away
   Towards the foothills grim and grey
That lead to Old Man's Town.

                Banjo Patterson 1902.

We'll send in the Oldies.

We mail the in-laws two plane tickets to come and visit for a fortnight.

They need a break. The world has been getting them down for so long. They carry their disappointment like a virus that they're trying to give to somebody else.

Take music for instance. No music can be just enjoyed without disparaging that other tuneless music which is presumably going on elsewhere, though I can't hear it.

Now they're complaining about the exhibition that's in town, the Guillaume collection, *Renoir to Picasso*, a random assortment to be sure, but that's beside the point.

As for aboriginal art what do you make of that, Eddie?

Well, they didn't paint it for you or me, Jack.

You see, Art creates the dialogue that a society has with itself.

Ah, you're talking nonsense.

It's all rubbish and you haven't the courage to say it.

And furthermore, the dialogue that it has with its gods and with posterity.

Who said that?

Me.

That's rubbish! You people always say the artist meant this and that. He was just painting what he saw, with no thought of posterity.

It doesn't matter what he was thinking, the world takes it out of his hands.

That's rubbish, what you said. The dictionary says: "Skill applied to imitation and—

DAMN THE DAMN DICTIONARY!

The music again. Old 1930s big band stuff.

And here comes the famous Bunny Berigan solo. You probably know it.

Marie

PAh, we had a guy in Ingham, Carl Hanson, he could knock spots off that. I can't hear any triple tonguing there

tri...

RIGHT! From here ON it's the Sex Pistols

(an illustration of the earlier point: music as society's generational dialogue.)

Old Man's Town. - page 2.

So why does it happen? Is it an inevitability we all must suffer? Must we all one day subscribe to the closed head policy?

That's it! Not a single one more!

Perhaps we perceive reality exactly as it is at one point of time only in our life.

Reality test: At what moment did I start thinking I'm a chess piece moved around by capricious gods?

Like the flexible mirror device for measuring the body image of obsessive slimmers. We arrive from concavity and bulge into convexity.

That's me. stop there.

Like drunkenness in which the point at which we know we've drunk too much alas corresponds exactly to the point at which we lose the will to do something about it.

Reality test: is an old folks home a quarantine facility?

Or is it a staging house, an ante-room to the better, safer, next world?

But God forfend a fate so dread
Alone to travel down
The dreary road we all
     must tread,
With faltering steps and
     whitening head,
The road to
     Old Man's Town!

Things have been getting me down lately. A cold sore blossoms on my lip overnight.

Eddie!

Come down here and help me get the beer out of the taxi!

WARF WARF WARF WARF WARF WARF WARF WARF

Old Man's Town - page 3.

152

Eddie

Nobody left at the Café Guerbois.

por
Edouard
Campbell
' 02.

In Paris we find ourselves in the *Pere Lachaise* cemetery.

At first it's just a cold big place where the dead people live.

And then it warms, becomes much more than that.

How could so much genius wind up in the same boneyard?

I feel at home.

Enjoying the posthumous company.

Chatting over "Fred" Chopin's nocturnes.

Tipping my *chapeau* to Theodore Gericault, lolling smugly on his stone.

I'll blow a big kiss to Oscar Wilde.

I'll prance around with Isadora, blow a couple of choruses with Mezz Mezzrow, whose primary skill, they say, was in getting hold of marijuana.

Georges Bizet, I've been meaning to ask... how far back does that tango rhythm go anyway?

Georges Melies, pardon me for using the moon-face in Snakes and Ladders.

Ah, Colette. 'L'Innocence Monstrevese' indeed.

Rest well, Abelard et Heloise, together toujours.

Au revoir, Honoré Daumier, Jacques Louis David, Eugene Delacroix.

Sisley and Pisarro, au revoir to you all.

Au revoir. I have a plane to catch.

Pere Lachaise - Page 2.

WALLYHOOD ENDING

Eddie Campbell
12/01

Here I am on my mission to Wallyhood. My name's on billboards and the sides of buses.

Hayley's buying her gear for the premiere

Go and find a pub, Dad. Come back later.

Twelve years ago I started drawing the book.

I finished Jackarippy. I go to bed now.

Frowning up from the cover of the free magazine at the entrance to the punky clothes store is Joe Strummer, still being punky twenty two years after I saw him at the Glasgow Apollo.

Do we all get to be cool for a second go-round?

I want you to give Robbie Coltrane a big squeeze and say it's from Pam.

I wasn't too fussed about coming all this way for the premiere.

I'll see Wallyhood, but will it see me?

You're so arrogant!

DAD! WE MUST GO!! YOU promised

I'm invisible on the red carpet.

Wallyhood Ending page 1

I originally imagined I'd get a bunch of pals together for the gala party, but such is not to be in the aftermath of Osama Bin Laden's attack on New York.

It's all tight security and paranoia now.

Ah, but fictions everywhere! Lolita is sitting behind me.

Dad! There's the guy from 'Dude, Where's my Car?'

Wait! Did I just see...?

Then the showdown, with... !SPOILER!... Ian Holm as the villainous Dr. Gull.

Johnny kisses Heather for the photographers.

No! It's a mask! It's... it's... MY NEMESIS!

Then, he scratches his head.

I'm Gary Cooper and it's High Noon.

Scene 58 ① Dramatic climax → SNOOTER REVEALED. (MUSIC) ② Pan Right — chase starts -

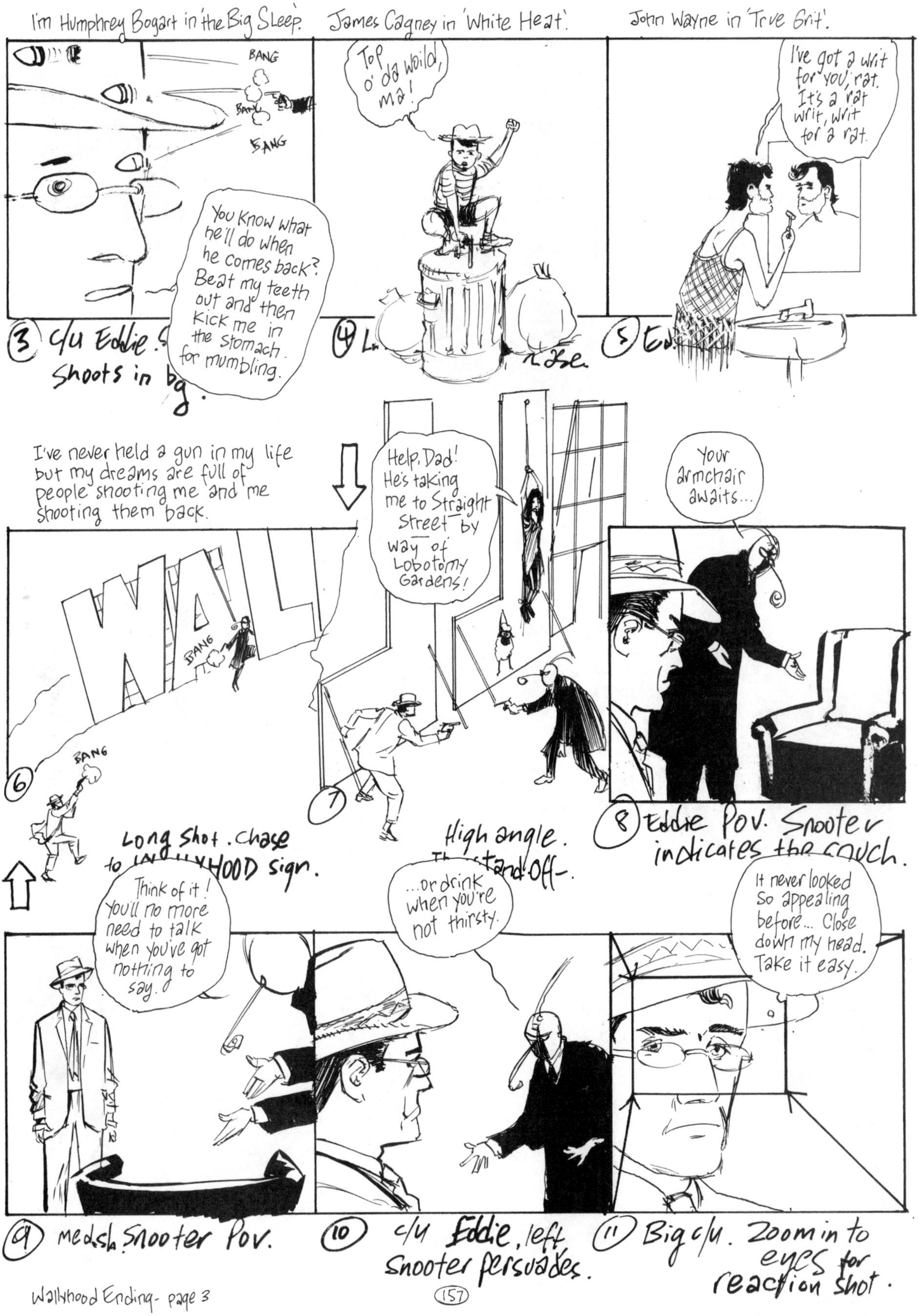
I'm Humphrey Bogart in 'the Big Sleep.'
BANG
BANG
BANG
You know what he'll do when he comes back? Beat my teeth out and then kick me in the stomach for mumbling.
3 C/U Eddie.
shoots in bg.
James Cagney in 'White Heat.'
Top o' da woild, ma!
4
John Wayne in 'True Grit'.
I've got a writ for you, rat. It's a rat writ, writ for a rat.
5
I've never held a gun in my life but my dreams are full of people shooting me and me shooting them back.
BANG
BANG
6
Long shot. Chase to
HOOD sign.
Help, Dad! He's taking me to Straight Street by way of Lobotomy Gardens!
7
High angle.
stand off.
Your armchair awaits...
8 Eddie Pov. Snooter indicates the couch.
Think of it! You'll no more need to talk when you've got nothing to say.
9 med.sh. Snooter Pov.
...or drink when you're not thirsty.
10 c/u Eddie, left Snooter persuades.
It never looked so appealing before... Close down my head. Take it easy.
11 Big c/u. Zoom in to eyes for reaction shot.

George Harrison dies at 58, perhaps the first of my generation's heroes to go in non-tragic circumstances.

And in a shop a particular bouquet of cheap newsprint transports me to a shop 35 years earlier.

Tomar-Re is saying something serious out of his funny beak.

I walk the dog just after the rain. Everything reminds me of something else.

All my friends advance a square in the big board game.

Two short TV spots taped in Paris.

I'm signing books in Madrid and Rome.

In Madrid I fall on my face.

I fall so hard I'm stunned

Wallyhood Ending · page 4

St. Louis Community College
at Meramec
Library

I'm still signing books on the Metro.

Then I find myself in a group photo.

St. Louis Community College
at Meramec
Library

Good night sweetheart

It's all for her.

Eddie Campbell
May 7 2002